MLM Blueprint

KODY BATEMAN

EAGLE ONE
PUBLISHING

www.eagleonepublishing.com

ISBN: 978-1-936677-05-4

Library of Congress Control Number: 2011942983

Cover design: Dave Baker, Baker Group Utah
Interior book design: Beth Watson, Watson Design Services
Interior illustrations: Ryan Tranmer
Publisher: Melody Marler Forshee

For information on purchasing bulk orders or on having this title customized for your company, please email the publisher at info@ eagleonepublishing.com. For more information about MLM Blueprint Workshop training and events, visit www.mlmblueprint.com.

Printed in the United States of America

EAGLE ONE
PUBLISHING

www.eagleonepublishing.com

PO Box 26173
Salt Lake City, UT 84126

For everyone who wants to live the life of their dreams, make a positive imprint on the world, and truly make the money they know they are capable of earning in the proud profession of network marketing.

Praise for *MLM Blueprint*

I first met Kody Bateman over 20 years ago. Even then, the ideas for the dynasty he has since created were percolating. He exuded an unstoppable entrepreneurial spirit. Kody is a man of principle, vision, purpose, and heart. The extraordinary success he has achieved, and thousands of lives he has changed in MLM, give him insights and clarity that uniquely qualify him to write this book. As I read *MLM Blueprint*, I was able to clearly identify when and how my own MLM blueprint changed from negative to positive. Phenomenal success quickly followed.

MLM Blueprint is a must-read for everyone in the MLM profession, and will lay the foundation for your success. Kody gets to the core of the issues and offers practical, actionable guidance. No matter where you are in your business right now, by implementing these strategies, you will rise to the greatness within you and break through any barriers that are holding you back.

**Margie Aliprandi, Network Marketing Professional,
International Speaker and Wealth Acceleration Coach**

In today's world, just about everyone has been touched by network marketing. Kody's *MLM Blueprint* book comes at the perfect time. Distributors need to develop professional skills, but those skills are worthless if they are built on a bad mental foundation. By writing this important book, Kody has done a tremendous service to everyone in network marketing. No serious distributor should be without it.

**Eric Worre, $15 Million Dollar Earner,
Creator of *Network Marketing Pro***

Contents

Foreword

I've been a network marketing professional for many years, and struggled for over 10 years in a number of companies without making a dime. Before Kody Bateman introduced his concept of the MLM Blueprint, I had never heard that phrase or given much thought to how I felt about MLM, even after I had become the top income-earner in my current company. As soon as I heard him speak about this topic, I felt an immediate shift in my thinking — an "aha" moment that would change how I would forever think and feel about MLM.

This book made me think back to another defining moment I had in 1993, one that changed my MLM blueprint and altered my future, even though I wasn't aware of it at the time. I was sitting around a table with the top five earners in my company and I had not even sponsored my first distributor. At the time, all of them were earning six figures per year. As I listened to the conversations among them, I noticed they were just like me. Two of them had family members who had rejected them. One of them had tried multiple programs and failed year after year. One of them worked the business for weeks before sponsoring his first distributor. Yet all of them had gone on to create five- and six-figure monthly incomes. I was just trying to put my finger on what they all had in common, and all of a sudden I realized I was just like them! If they could do it, then I could too — I just had to believe that I could. I had to let go of what other people thought, what other people did, and just focus on how I thought and felt about MLM, and what I believed could be true for me.

This represented a fundamental shift in my MLM blueprint, although I didn't have a name for this massive adjustment at the time. I went from buying macaroni and cheese at three boxes for a dollar and taking the bus to work to having primary residences in four different cities, leasing private jets, and walking the beaches of the world. My transformed blueprint allowed me to create a foundation that has supported a journey of growth that has now spanned almost two decades.

Now keep in mind, I didn't sponsor a single distributor in my first 10 years as a network marketing professional. I told myself I wanted to be successful, but had a blueprint that was keeping me from it. I would get excited about a company, sign up, share my opportunity with a few of my friends and family, and WHAM! I would get blasted with a shot of cynicism from one of my closest friends, or my hottest prospect would stop returning my calls. That's all it would take and I would be wounded, discouraged, and out of business. Typically within my first two weeks, I had quit the company that I had declared to be my current ticket to financial success. I did this over and over again with 11 separate companies over a 10-year period.

When I finally started paying attention to how I actually felt about network marketing, identifying blocks and changing my beliefs about myself and about this profession, everything changed for me. Once my MLM blueprint changed, I went on to make over $14 million in the next 15 years. All those obstacles that held me back for so many years no longer existed in my world. My business is now built on a solid foundation that gives me the beliefs and habits necessary to thrive regardless of my circumstances.

MLM Blueprint breaks it all down and puts a name to this struggle, familiar to so many in network marketing. It will require you to do a deep dive into your past exposures to network marketing. It may be painful, but do the exercises. You may learn, like I did, that you are just like those successful top income-earners. And if they can do it, and I can do it, then you can do it too.

It's not the product or the compensation plan that will determine your success. In every company there are big earners, and there are also many who struggle. It's not circumstances or obstacles that hold anyone back. In every case, a top performer will rise through the ranks of a company regardless of their product, compensation plan, circumstances, or obstacles. Why? Because they have a solid MLM blueprint, which provides them the resources to excel.

At a recent company incentive trip, I was sitting poolside under a colorful umbrella at a resort in Orlando with a group of seasoned network marketing professionals. I asked, "What percent of the population believes that $100,000 per month is too good to be true?" Most everyone there agreed that about 97% of the general population believes that $100,000 per month sounds too good to be true. I then asked, "Of the 3% that doesn't believe it's too good to be true, what percent of those think it's too good to be true **for them**?" As a group we determined that only a fraction of those think that it's even possible for them. Until one believes that it's possible for them, they won't commit to do the work necessary to create it. You can see why so many handicap themselves with this belief — why it's hard for some people to actually go on to make a lot of money in network marketing.

Once my blueprint was strengthened to include the belief that $100,000 per month was a real possibility for me, I began to acquire the skills, meet the right people, and align myself with the resources necessary to bring forth that result in my life. My MLM blueprint has been the pivotal component in the creation of my MLM success. I had to acknowledge the state of my own MLM blueprint, adjust it, and I work every day to keep it in positive alignment with the life of my dreams.

I now realize *Beach Money* is a book that I wrote to help alter someone's MLM blueprint so that they had a shot at success. *MLM Blueprint* will help everyone in this profession, whether they are brand new to MLM or have been working in network marketing for years, discover their defining moments, and help them live the life of their dreams. Congratulations for picking up this book. Do the work, and we'll see you on the beach!

Jordan Adler, Network Marketing Professional and
bestselling author of Beach Money™:
Creating Your Dream Life Through Network Marketing

Introduction

The idea of an MLM blueprint took form in my mind a few years ago during a coaching call with one of my network marketing company's distributors. This distributor's success had plateaued, causing him anxiety and frustration and leaving him with the feeling of wanting to abandon his MLM business. Through a series of questions, I was able to help him discover his block and, in the process, uncover the framework for this book and the *MLM Blueprint Workshop*.

For the past couple years, I've dedicated myself to the study of the MLM blueprint and the subconscious. If you've picked up this book, I'm betting you are either involved in or interested in joining a multilevel (network marketing) opportunity, and want to make the best start possible.

Our profession is referred to with those two names, and they're often interchangeable. I purposely chose to title this book *MLM Blueprint* because so many people assign negativity to MLM references. This negativity can be reframed, however, and I'll explain how. The same people who automatically frame MLM opportunities in a negative mindset also come from a cynical world, and they are exposed to negativity the majority of the time. The cynical people in this negative world think MLM is a business where people try to recruit you so they can make money from your efforts. The fact is, MLM is a business where someone recruits you to help you elevate to a better and more positive way of life.

I am someone who absolutely loves network marketing. One of the reasons I love network marketing is because it delivers personal development at its very best. It creates an environment where an individual can step out of his or her world of negativity and be around like-minded, positive people. It also provides financial opportunities to the masses with the built-in support of people, referred to as an upline, who have a vested interest in that individual's success.

Since founding my own global network marketing company, where I currently serve as CEO, we have signed up and worked with over 140,000 distributors and 300,000 customers of our products, generated more than $60 million in commissions, and brought in more than $250 million in revenue. I started this business as a distributor and built the downline in a grassroots effort, primarily from warm-market prospecting using my own and a partner's warm-market lists—the same way I ask new distributors to build theirs. We never cut any deals with MLM leaders of other companies, nor did we initiate any growth from an influx of distributors joining our team from other organizations.

As an individual with a downline to support, I have learned amazing things about human behavior, as well as what does and doesn't work in building a network marketing organization. Most importantly, I have learned that a personal development plan that nourishes the subconscious is the single most important element to achieving success in this or any business. From the beginning of my own network marketing company, I developed and taught a full-day personal development seminar to our new representatives as part of our company's offerings; many take the course over and over again. When people join us in this business, most of them have a glimmer of hope in their eyes—a hope for a better future. That glimmer is a tremendous responsibility to a network marketing company and to any distributor building a team. We take that responsibility very seriously and teach our distributors to do the same.

Many of these people just joining a network marketing company, however, don't even realize their hope may be unconsciously mired with negative thoughts about their chosen profession. In this book, I hope to help others recognize the negative imprints they may be unconsciously allowing into their subconscious. This book will give everyone the tools to replace those negative imprints with positive imprints, creating a foundation to help create a blueprint for MLM success.

AN "AHA" MOMENT

One morning a few years ago, I started my daily routine, which began with returning phone calls and emails from people in my organization. This particular morning, I received a phone call from a distributor who did not have an active sponsor or upline. This person had reached our second rank advancement and was making on average about $1,500 per month; in his biggest month, he had earned $3,500. He asked if I would take some time to help him through some of his frustrations. He'd hit a wall and could not seem to keep his business growing.

I asked him a series of questions about how he was working his business. It appeared he was doing all the right things. He was using the prospect and follow-up systems, running presentations correctly, using the right tools, and promoting the company and distributor events. This was part of the reason for his frustration. All those things seemed to work great for him as he built his way to his current income level. But at that level, he simply hit a wall—as if everything quit working. He had people falling off (attrition), and he was struggling to maintain the team he had grown.

If you've been in this business for a while, you can probably relate to this experience.

I was running through questions in my mind, wondering how I could help him. As I exhausted my questions, I realized I didn't have an answer for him. Then a thought came to me. I had been reading and studying the works of T. Harv Eker, author of *Secrets of the Millionaire Mind*. He shares a concept he calls "money blueprints," the idea that we all have an established blueprint in our subconscious about money. According to Eker, our blueprints work like a thermostat; he believes we have subconsciously established a set amount of money that we think we are worth, or that we think we are capable of earning. We also have set beliefs about money, and we manifest those beliefs into our reality.

For example, if a person associates with or lives around people who make less than $3,000 per month, and he is used to making less than $3,000 per month, chances are his blueprint or thermostat is set at less than $3,000 per month. Once he hits $3,000 in monthly income, the thermostat shuts off, and he doesn't make more than that amount. Eker shares examples of how people who are used to making a set amount lose their source of income, get a new source of income, and almost always get back to that set amount quickly—but rarely do they move beyond it. He goes on to explain how we can change the setting on our money thermostat and begin to manifest more income.

Still on the phone with my friend, I was excited by this thought and figured I had the answer to his dilemma. Certainly he must have a money blueprint set at around $3,500 per month. This would explain everything. With a smug sense of being a guru who was about to change this guy's life, I excitedly asked my next question.

"How long have you been working professionally?"

He said, "About 20 years."

Next question: "How many jobs or ventures have you done in that 20 years?"

"Three jobs and a few business ventures," he answered.

Now I was going in for the kill. I asked, "What was the average amount of monthly income you made at those jobs and ventures?" I thought for sure he was going to say around $3,500.

He said, "Well that's just it. I am used to making great income at everything I do. My average income at my last job was well over $15,000 per month, and I have probably averaged $10,000 per month in income for 20 years."

Ouch! So much for being a guru. Now what was I going to say to him? This guy had an excellent money blueprint. He had achieved great success in his professional life. His father and family members had been very successful in professional ventures. Why had he not been able to earn more than $3,500 per month in his MLM business?

Right then, the **real** "aha!" moment came: I needed to ask him about his MLM experience. Maybe his money blueprint was strong, but he had hang-ups about MLM. If we have money blueprints, is it possible we also have an MLM blueprint? After all, I personally know many successful people who have tried their hand in MLM and failed miserably.

So I began a new line of questioning, asking him about his history and experiences with MLM, or network marketing.

Question number 1: *Prior to your current MLM venture, had you ever done another MLM, and how much did you make?* He answered that he had never done an MLM himself—this was his first venture.

Question number 2: *Prior to your current MLM venture, what was the highest amount anyone you personally knew made in MLM?* He said he didn't know anyone who had made any money in MLMs. In fact, he said he had avoided MLMs because he thought they were sketchy. And the people he knew who had tried them usually quit within the first year or two.

It appeared this conversation was now going somewhere. Think about it. He had no previous MLM experience himself, he didn't know anyone who made any money in MLM, and the people he did know usually quit within the first couple years. Was it possible his subconscious was telling him it was time to quit? Not only was that possible, it's exactly what happened. The power of the subconscious is amazing.

This experience launched my interest into studying the MLM blueprint, and discovering that blueprint and its associated imprints can possibly be the single biggest asset or liability to a person's success in this business. If it is possible to redefine your current money blueprint, resetting it to the level you desire, is it also possible to do the same with your MLM blueprint? Could it be the missing key to dramatically help the 92 percent who fail in this business? As an owner of a network marketing company with a downline of more than 100,000 people, I was very interested to find out. Even in my own downline, why was it that the top 10 percent of income earners made more than the other 90 percent combined? How can we help thousands of people in this business get to the level of income they need and desire? Being both a personal development teacher and student, I immediately began to explore the possibilities of a workshop or course that could help people improve their MLM blueprint.

REFRAMING THE IDEA OF MULTILEVEL MARKETING

In his book, Eker explains that studies have shown that the word "money" invokes more negative emotion than any other single word. He jokingly says that's because most people don't have enough of it. Common sense tells me that in the business world, the term *multilevel marketing* or *MLM* invokes more negative emotion than most words. Because this is a warm-market business, most people hear about an MLM opportunity from someone who is close to them. Most of the people who tell them negative things about an MLM have failed in one; not only do they hear the story, but they feel the emotion of the failure. A blueprint of failure imprints on the subconscious. And people don't even know it's happening. As a profession, we have a responsibility to free people from negative MLM blueprints that are holding them back in this business.

Since the phone call where I had that "aha" moment, I have written about and conducted the *MLM Blueprint Workshop* several times with extraordinary results. I have found that it is relatively simple to change, enhance, and strengthen your MLM blueprint; in fact, it's essential to your success in this business. The stories you have in your subconscious are the stories you end up living. You can take control of your MLM story and make it a success story. And if you follow the systems and use the tools provided by your company, you will find yourself being recognized on the stage and cashing the big checks.

This book began with the exploration of my own MLM history and evaluation of the strength of my own blueprint. I then compared my experience to others and coupled those discoveries with personal development training I have conducted for several years, which involves nourishment of the subconscious. I studied the process of how blueprints are created and what they are used for. In the process, I discovered some striking similarities between how a blueprint is created and used to build structures and how we create blueprints in our subconscious, which manifest or build into reality. Most importantly, I created a way for you to visualize the blueprints you have created around your MLM story. Through that visualization, you can create awareness and pursue positive change.

The stories in your mind truly do become the stories of your life. What you think and feel is what you manifest. *MLM Blueprint* will help you unearth and analyze the stories you have built, and you'll discover how they are affecting your MLM business. *MLM Blueprint* will also show you how to create stories that will be in complete alignment with massive MLM success. Everything in your MLM career changes for the better now!

CHAPTER 1

Blueprints and the Subconscious

The most familiar type of blueprint is the plan used in architectural or engineering renderings that acts as the framework for a construction crew. Blueprints are usually made on paper with several layers outlining the various processes used to create something, most often a building or structure.

Historically, blueprints were made using chemically coated paper that was placed under a translucent original drawing and exposed to intensely bright light. After being exposed, the chemical treatment was then washed off, leaving the desired imprint of the original drawing on the paper. This process, discovered in the early 18th century, was the preferred method of creating blueprints until nearly the end of the 20th century.

Today, the actual blueprinting process no longer happens this way, as computer and photocopy technology have simplified the process. The term blueprint, however, is still used to describe a detailed building plan. And the process still begins with paper being exposed, leaving the desired imprint of the tracing from the computer-generated drawing on the paper.

The thought process behind creating a building structure always starts with a detailed set of plans. With exposures, the blueprint is imprinted with a foundation plan, a flooring plan, and a framing plan. These three imprinted plans are used together to create the shell of the structure. When the building is finished, you will never see the shell again. All the remaining imprinted plans are designed and used to build onto the shell of the structure. These plans represent things you can always see, such as the finished interior and exterior of the building.

The following illustration is a highly simplified visual of how these imprinted plans might be layered. You will notice the foundational imprints first, layered in the proper order and moving upward until the shell is completed. This is the critical part of the structure you do not see. The finished imprinted plans are then

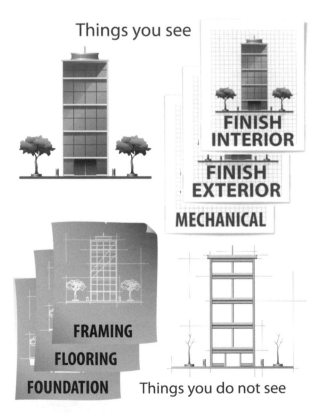

layered on top of the foundational imprints, representing the finished product—the building elements you can see.

Recently we were staying with a group of friends at my mountain cabin. While discussing this blueprinting concept, I asked one friend to look at an interior wall in the cabin. It covered two levels and was finished with tongue-and-groove pinewood. I then asked him to look at the ceiling. It was finished with the same thing. I asked him how he thought that wall and ceiling were built. Thinking I was only talking about what he could see, he figured precut tongue-and-groove pieces of pinewood were brought in and stacked on top of each other.

"How does it stay up?" I asked him.

"Well, I'm sure it's applied to some kind of framing that's behind it," he said. "And the framing has to match up with the dimensions we are looking at."

If you are sitting in a room as you read these words, stop and look around the room. What do you notice? You probably see the finish elements of the structure you are sitting in. You see finished walls around you. There is a finished ceiling above your head. You are standing or sitting on a finished floor beneath you. Imagine attempting to erect what you are looking at without having the foundational shell designed to hold the structure. Perhaps the doors and windows of your shell are in different places, or the dimensions of your shell are smaller or larger than what you are looking at. You simply cannot build a structure without first having a foundational shell that's in alignment with the parts you see.

After learning the original process of how a blueprint was created (with exposures and imprints) and how blueprints are used to create a building (with layered imprints), I was struck by the similarities between that imprinting process and how our subconscious and conscious minds work.

Everything we manifest in our lives comes from the subconscious. The subconscious does not think. It feels. The conscious mind does your thinking and continually sends those thoughts to your subconscious. The subconscious acts like a sponge, soaking in every thought, good and bad. It accepts what you send it as if it is real. That's the challenge most people encounter living in a world where the majority of things we are exposed to is negative. That means we are constantly processing negative information, and our subconscious soaks it all up. The subconscious is not capable of originating a thought. It simply processes the conscious mind's thoughts, producing the emotions those thoughts generate. The more you dwell on the emotion of the thought, the stronger the imprint on the subconscious. And these imprints are creating your blueprint.

What we manifest or create in our lives begins with our minds receiving *exposures*—our real-life experiences. The mind interprets these experiences into thoughts, and those thoughts in turn create *imprints* on our subconscious. Those imprints are layered on top of each other in the order of imagination, beliefs, and habits. These are things you can't see, and they make up your inner shell. Although we can't actually see the imprints of our imagination, beliefs, and habits, we feel them, we dream them, and we manifest our conscious lives by them. They represent the very things that manifest what you see as reality. In other words, your subconscious shell is what everything you *can* see in your life is built upon.

Those things you can see are represented by the information you receive, the experiences you live, and the lifestyle you create.

Ultimately, this is your conscious life. Here is what this might look like in comparison to a structural building blueprint.

In the format of a blueprint, this illustration shows how your mind works. Everything that goes into the mind begins with an

CONSCIOUS

Things you see

LIFESTYLE

EXPERIENCES

INFORMATION

HABITS

BELIEFS

IMAGINATION

SUBCONSCIOUS

Things you
do not see

exposure from the world in which we live. That exposure creates a thought that imprints the imagination, forms beliefs, and creates habits. The subconscious imprinting that rules your life is powered by the exposures you have and the thoughts you have about those exposures. If you imprint your subconscious with negative thoughts, they will build a negative foundation. And since your imagination magnifies whatever thought you send it, if negativity is going in, your imagination will intensify that negativity. This will cause negative beliefs to be imprinted, and habits that support those beliefs are formed. As a result, you attract negative information, manifest negative experiences, and create an undesired lifestyle. It becomes a vicious cycle because it will attract more negative exposures to your life experience. This is like building a structure on a weak foundation—it makes it very difficult for your desired finished structure to stand.

On the other hand, if you imprint your subconscious with positive thoughts, you will build a positive foundation. Your imagination will magnify the positivity. A strong belief system will be imprinted, and solid habits supporting those beliefs will be formed. As a result, you will attract positive information, manifest positive experiences, and create the lifestyle of your dreams. This becomes a positive cycle as you attract more positive exposures to your life experience. Since your subconscious does not know the difference between what is real or imagined, it believes whatever you expose it to. The higher the intensity of the emotion, good or bad, the more it believes and the more quickly it manifests.

A few years ago, I wrote a song titled "Stories" about the stories we put in our mind becoming the stories we live out in our lives. A portion of the lyrics goes like this:

> *You get to choose the stories in your mind,*
> *Good or bad only you can find.*
> *They're never real when they begin,*
> *It's up to me if I lose or win.*

Some are good, some are bad,
Imagination makes us happy or sad.

Think about those lyrics. The stories we create are never real when they begin, regardless of where they come from. If your exposure is negative and your thoughts entertain that negativity, your imagination magnifies or intensifies that negativity. A story is created in your subconscious, and beliefs and habits are formed to support that story. You then manifest that story into your conscious world. A foundational blueprint is created and can only manifest negative results in your conscious world.

Here's a fictitious example: Your Uncle Joe was your basketball coach when you were 12 years old. He taught you the fundamentals of the game and helped you create positive stories about your abilities on the basketball court. He was a mentor and role model—someone you looked up to. Uncle Joe was a great coach, but he always had challenges with his finances. He had a hard time holding down a job, and he never seemed to make ends meet. You used to hear him say things like, "Money is not easy to come by," "You will never be able to afford that," or "If people are making lots of money, they are probably ripping somebody off."

Because Uncle Joe was a mentor, you hung on his every word when you were a kid. He was unknowingly providing you with negative exposures about money. Your thoughts mimicked his thoughts. They were negative on the subject of money, and your imagination magnified those thoughts. A negative story was created in your subconscious about money, and then negative beliefs and habits were formed around money. As a result, you may have now spent years of your life manifesting negative thoughts about money; without even knowing it, you created a negative blueprint about money. The story in your mind became the story of your life.

I made up this story about Uncle Joe to illustrate how the mind works—without us even realizing what's happening. Unfortunately, this sort of thing happens every day to millions of people. It may have even struck a chord with your own experiences around money. If it did, chances are you are working from a negative blueprint about money.

Let's use another fictitious example about Uncle Joe, but this time with MLM as the source of the exposure. Your Uncle Joe tells you that MLM is bad, illegal, immoral, and wrong. He even gives you an example of an MLM company that was recently shut down because of illegal practices. This becomes your exposure, and you entertain this exposure with negative thoughts about MLM. You imprint your imagination with that negativity, and your imagination magnifies that story. Beliefs and habits begin to form that support this negative story, and you ultimately manifest negative experiences with MLM. Again, without even knowing it, you've created a negative blueprint about MLM and are now manifesting negative results with your MLM business.

What I have found through teaching the *MLM Blueprint Workshop* is that this type of story really happens to many people, and it blocks them from having success in their MLM businesses.

Why? It's very simple: People get into an MLM with the hope of being successful. They want the finished structure of their life experience to be one of financial prosperity and time freedom. The problem is, their foundational structure is not in alignment with those desires. Instead, the foundation was built to support the bad stories or failures of MLM. As hard as they try, they are not able to build the finished structure they desire because their subconscious will not allow it. In other words, their MLM blueprint is messed up. The good news is that if you understand the blueprint process, you can quickly shift this kind of negative exposure. You will soon find you have complete control of the imprinting process going on in your brain.

Try our fictitious example now, knowing that you have control over the imprinting process: Your Uncle Joe tells you that MLM is bad, illegal, immoral, and wrong. He even gives you an example of an MLM company that was recently shut down because of illegal practices. This is a story Uncle Joe planted in your mind when you were a kid. It remained in your memory, and up to this point, it has had a negative impact, whether you realized it or not, on your thoughts about MLM.

But you are now an adult, and you want to establish a career in network marketing. Because of your awareness of the MLM blueprint process, you have already aligned your thinking  with positive information about MLM. Through this process, you have recalled the "Uncle Joe exposure" from your memory. At this point, you now know you have a choice. You can allow Uncle Joe's story to continue creating the imprint on your imagination, or you can establish your own story. In fact, you have even learned about the company your uncle told you about—the one that was shut down—but now you know why. Through your own research into MLM, you learned that even though that one company fell apart due to illegal practices, there are another hundred MLM companies that abide by the law for every one that does not—a percentage similar to companies from numerous other industries. You focus on the company you are involved with and have confidence that it supplies an enormous value to the marketplace with its products and opportunity.

This change of focus is easier said than done. Typically, the "Uncle Joe" stories have been collecting in your subconscious over the years. A whole lot of imprinting has happened. Even though you know you can shift the process with your own exposures, you still have to correct the old foundational imprinting that has happened. The key is repetition of positive exposures.

These past experiences are known as **historical exposures**. It's important to explore your historical exposures because they have created the foundational blueprints you could be using to build your network marketing career. The information, experiences, and lifestyle you are manifesting (things you see in your life) are always in alignment with what has gone on in your imagination, your beliefs, and your habits (things you don't see in the subconscious). Again, the good news is you can discover these historical exposures and correct them if you need to. As the lyrics of the song say, "You get to choose the stories in your mind, good or bad only you can find."

CONSCIOUS

Things you see

LIFESTYLE
EXPERIENCES
INFORMATION

Many personal development students have figured out how to rewrite stories in their mind with affirmations. I like to refer to affirmations as "I am" statements, because if you state in present tense the

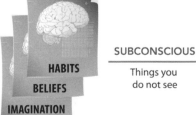

SUBCONSCIOUS

Things you
do not see

HABITS
BELIEFS
IMAGINATION

things you desire, the subconscious acts as if these are already real. This is the very reason the stories you create in your mind become the stories you live in your life. The challenge most people have with this is they don't realize when their conscious exposures oppose their affirmation efforts. If your daily information or thoughts do not align with the imagination or belief plans you worked so hard to establish, your desired manifestations are not going to line up.

If someone initiates the imagination and verbalizes an affirmation that says, "I am financially independent and free," he takes control of an exposure that places a desired imprint on his imagination. His imagination immediately begins to magnify a feel-good emotion around financial independence.

But then he initiates information and thoughts around his lack of money, habitually using language like, "I can't afford to buy a new car." Here's what will happen: A new, negative "I am" statement or affirmation was created—"I can't afford to buy a new car"—and it was imprinted right over the top of the positive one you intended, which said, "I am financially independent and free." Negative statements tend to overpower positive ones because most people expose their subconscious to far more negative influences than they do positive. This is the reason positive affirmations do not work for many people; they state a desired affirmation but allow their daily language to "throw up" all over it.

The reality is that affirmations or "I am" statements always work. The statements you think and verbalize the most are the statements that manifest. The stories you put into your mind are the stories you end up living in your life.

I share this universal law for one simple reason. If you simply review the historical exposures you have had around MLM, you can quickly see the positive stories that are serving you and the negative ones keeping you from MLM success. Once you discover those exposures in your memory, you can use those that serve you and rewrite those that don't.

Uncle Joe said, "Money is not easy to come by."

You now say, "I am attracting wealth in abundance."

Uncle Joe said, "MLM is bad, illegal, immoral, and wrong."

You now say, "My MLM business provides an enormous value to the marketplace."

The next fictitious example is known as a **current exposure**—what you are experiencing today. For example, let's say you get involved with an MLM opportunity. You decide to test the waters and see if your closest friend will join you. You call her, explain what you are doing, and she proceeds to shut you down. She tells you how disappointed she is that you would get involved with something like this. She is upset because you approached her with it. This is an unwanted reaction from your outside world. You immediately reinforce that experience with your thoughts, and feel-bad emotions are attached to them. You feel hurt and unprepared; your imagination is imprinted and runs wild, creating an immediate belief that MLM doesn't work. You quit.

This is an example that prematurely ends the efforts of millions of people taking a quick run at making money with MLM. Without even knowing it, these people allowed someone else's thoughts about MLM to create a blueprint in their minds. Because so many emotions are involved, the exposure burns deep and becomes very difficult to fix. This experience acts as a shutdown, and the best way to fix it is to avoid it altogether. How do you do that? You simply create an awareness of the MLM blueprint process, and you prepare yourself for these kinds of exposures.

Here's one way to get prepared for the possibility of shutdowns: You get involved with an MLM opportunity. You get excited about it. You direct your thoughts toward your imagination, and you explore the possibilities this opportunity can provide you and your family. Emotions are attached to those thoughts, and positive imprints begin to form in your subconscious. They create an internal belief that your ship has come in. It feels good. You seek out information and experiences that will support those feelings. You are strengthened with training from your upline and your company. You understand that due to bad timing or their own preconceived beliefs, some will join you and others won't. And since you know this going in, you're okay with it. You have learned about the law of averages, and you are prepared for it with a little acronym that goes like this: SW, SW, SW, Next (Some will, some won't, so what? Next!). This helps you with two crucial things: It helps you to not take shutdowns personally, and it prepares you to work the law of averages to your advantage. The more people you talk to about your MLM, the less effect shutdowns will have on you.

Here's the previous example again, but this time you're prepared: You test the waters and see if your closest friend will join you. You call her, explain what you are doing, and she proceeds to shut you down. She tells you how disappointed she is that you would get involved with something like this. She is upset because you approached her with it. This is an unwanted reaction from your outside world. You feel temporary defeat but realize this is part of the game. You walk away with the law of averages in mind, with perspective and optimism. Your friend sees you are happy and confident about what you are doing. You continue as close friends, and she silently watches you from a distance to see how you are succeeding in your business. You have no worries because you know the day might come when she will be ready. Either way, it's OK. You simply move on to the next person on your list and keep building.

Thoughts and emotions are really the key to making this process work for or against you. Your thoughts create the emotion, which imprints on the subconscious. The subconscious manifests its most dominant feelings. It's important here to note there are really only two kinds of emotion: One feels good and the other feels bad. One is faith-based and the other is fear-based. If you understand and work with the law of averages, you maintain faith-based, feel-good emotions. If you are talking to enough people about your opportunity and doing it the right way, you will attract interested and positive people. That creates the feel-good emotions you need to feed your imagination. Your imagination will magnify those feelings, and positive beliefs and habits will naturally materialize. This is what successful people in network marketing do. This type of person is taking control of her exposures. She is making sure the subconscious has positive exposures on an ongoing basis.

Once again, "I am" statements can and should be used to control your current exposures to MLM. Your prospect says, "I can't believe you joined an MLM. Are you crazy?" You say, "I am successfully using the law of averages to live my dreams."

MLM BLUEPRINTS

So what is an MLM blueprint and how is it created? Whether you know it or not, you have an MLM blueprint established in your subconscious. That blueprint is currently determining the rate of success or failure of your MLM business efforts.

Your MLM blueprint was likely created by information and experiences you have had with MLM. You have generated emotions around those thoughts and stored memories. The combination of your emotions and memories has created imprints on your subconscious. As a result, you have triggered your imagination about MLM and created a set of beliefs and possibly even habits on the subject of MLM. Most people don't even know these things are being stored in their memory banks and imprinted on their subconscious. Even if you have properly created an MLM blueprint, you still face the challenge of daily negativity.

As an example, let's say you verbalize an affirmation that says, "I am making $100,000 per month in my MLM business." Your conscious sends that message to your subconscious, where a positive emotion places the desired imprint that you are a $100,000-per-month income earner.

Then you are subsequently exposed to information that challenges your ideas about MLMs: You then translate that exposure into language like, "I can't get my business to take off," or "I don't think my compensation plan works." Those conscious thoughts are sent to your subconscious, where a negative emotion places an undesired imprint for MLM failure. It is layered over the imprint for $100,000-per-month MLM success. The imprints do not align, so the blueprint for MLM success is weakened. You'll learn more about the power of the imagination, the value of affirmations (or "I am" statements) and the importance of everyday positive language, in Chapter 6.

CHAPTER 2

Historical Exposures

Most of us have had a series of exposures to MLM throughout our lives. I was very fortunate to have highly positive exposures through my experiences and subsequently from the information I gathered on my own. I later learned my imagination played a big part in those experiences, which left a positive imprint. As a result, I nourished my imagination and created highly positive affirmations around success in MLM. Because of this, I have acquired a strong and powerful blueprint for MLM success.

I'd like to share with you my own historical exposures to MLM. I did this by going back as far as my memory would take me. I wrote down each experience and the information I retained from that experience. Those memories helped me expose what I have imprinted on my subconscious about MLM. Just a little later in this chapter, you'll be guided through the same process.

FIRST EXPOSURE TO MLM

My first exposure to MLM happened in 1978, when I was 14 years old. A friend and I were riding our BMX bikes through a subdivided neighborhood, and we started talking about someone who lived in that neighborhood who appeared to have a lot of money. My friend told me he heard the man was on top of a money-pyramid thing where he made a percentage from the sales of thousands of people who were in the pyramid. He also heard we could join it, but he didn't know if it was legal or not. That's all I remember, but it must have registered subconsciously because I do remember the conversation, and that memory has surfaced many times in my life. At the time, it invoked an emotion of excitement around the possibility of making lots of money.

SECOND EXPOSURE TO MLM

My second exposure to MLM was when I was 22 years old, in the summer of 1986. I was home from college, working for my dad's company, earning money to go back for the fall semester. I went with one of my brothers to a job where we were finishing the basement of a large custom home in an affluent neighborhood. I remember being on a ladder, hanging a light fixture—something I did not enjoy doing. The owner of the home came through to check on things. He had a discussion with my brother and then left. I was blown away by how young this guy was. When he left, I asked my brother who he was and what he did for a living. My brother told me the homeowner's name was Craig Tillotson, and he did something with vitamins or skin care—my brother wasn't exactly sure what it was, but Craig made money selling these products. He also made money from the sales of those he recruited to sell the products. That was it. I don't remember my brother saying anything about it being an MLM or network marketing, but I do remember him saying we could join if we wanted.

THIRD EXPOSURE TO MLM

My very first invitation to an MLM came in 1989, when I was 25, and it was from my older brother Kris. This was in the late '80s when A.L. Williams was at critical mass. At that time, I knew nothing about A.L. Williams, and I had no clue what the term critical mass meant. What I did know was that my brother was excited about a philosophy of buying term life insurance. He was going to meetings that he wanted me to join, and he saw this as a way to make the kind of money that, as an electrical contractor, he could only dream of. I saw the light of hope in my brother's eyes. He was in his late 20s with a wife and three small children and was facing a real crossroads in his occupation. His entire life, Kris had worked for our father's electrical contracting company, which was now on the verge of closing its doors. Kris had always been our dad's right-hand guy. He took care of all the logistics of running the business. The challenge he had was that he'd never received any formal training in the electrical trade. Because of this, he was not overly marketable, and his likelihood of getting a job with another company was slim.

Kris needed to find another means of income, and this life-insurance thing coupled with a business opportunity seemed to be a solution. At the time, he did not mention to me that it was an MLM. I'm not even sure he knew it was. I simply remember how excited he was about it.

Kris and his wife bought a life-insurance policy from this company, and he began to work this venture as a part-time business. I was interested in what he was doing, but I was just finishing my bachelor's degree in marketing and had accepted an intern position at a large ad agency in New York City. It wasn't long after this that Kris, while still working his full-time job as an electrician, was electrocuted on a routine service call. His life was tragically cut short.

One of my final memories of my brother was his enthusiasm for his A.L. Williams business venture. That memory had a lasting impact on me. Kris was never able to realize his dream of building that venture. Financial freedom was very important to Kris. He had big dreams, and he wanted to make sure his family was taken care of.

I learned very little if anything about MLM with this exposure, but I registered a positive emotion about its possibilities. In fact, as I look back, I realize a positive seed was planted in my subconscious. The emotions of hope and possibility were imprinted, and MLM was part of that imprint.

FOURTH EXPOSURE TO MLM

My second invitation to MLM came when I was 28 years old, in 1992. I was working in Salt Lake City as director of marketing for a food-service company. A coworker invited me to attend a luncheon where some guy was doing a presentation on how to make lots of money. He offered to buy me lunch if I went. I accepted the invitation. We went to the restaurant and were seated in a large dining room. The guy running the meeting introduced himself as Nathan Ricks, an independent distributor for a company called Nu Skin International. He started to draw circles on a large whiteboard, explaining a process called duplication. He said if you sponsored five people into this business, and they sponsored five and so on through numerous levels, you'd end up with thousands of people in what he called a *downline*. This is the first time I had heard this term.

Nathan went on to explain that if each of those people purchased $100 per month worth of products and you made a small percentage off all of those purchases, you could potentially make hundreds of thousands of dollars every month. Wow! This was the first time I had seen the duplication presentation, and I immediately got it. This MLM thing was really cool. Now here was the kicker. He then said, "Our number-one income earner makes $500,000 per month. His name is Craig Tillotson."

I instantly remembered who Craig Tillotson was. He was the same guy I met five years earlier when we were working on finishing the basement of his huge home. I was amazed and excited; I was hooked. Although I didn't realize it at the time, these exposures were creating a blueprint in my subconscious about the power and possibilities of MLM. After that meeting, it seemed everywhere I went I heard exciting things about MLM opportunities. I ended up joining what appeared to be a spin-off of Nu Skin known as Images. That name was later changed to Neways.

After attending several training meetings, I learned Neways had a very limited amount of marketing tools available to present their product and opportunity. Having a background in marketing and collateral development, I put together some mock-up brochure presentations and showed them to the top distributor leaders. They loved them and encouraged me to produce the brochures and sell them directly to distributors. I created a few marketing pieces that were a big hit and got the attention of the number-one earner in that business. She and several other high-level distributors invited me to work with them on several projects.

This was great exposure for me. I was immediately exposed to the daily life of top-level distributors in MLM. I saw how they worked, usually from home; I witnessed their lifestyles; and I was exposed to a positive atmosphere as they listened to tapes and read personal development books. I even saw some of the downside to being in an MLM business, but the upside outweighed it by so much, even that excited me. All of this was further strengthening my thought process about the power of MLM.

Keep in mind, I was doing all of this part-time. I still held my full-time job as a marketing director. I was making enough money with my side MLM ventures to pay off some personal debt and move my family into our first home. I continued to see more and more opportunities to supply support services to MLM companies and their distributors. I was amazed at how much time distributors spent on the phone. They were spending lots of money on long-distance and voicemail service, and top leaders were spending even more on conference-call services where they could talk to hundreds of people at a time. I saw an opportunity to supply telecommunication services to distributors of network marketing companies. I knew very little about telecommunications, but a lot about what distributors were looking for in that service. I connected with a reseller of long-distance service who offered independent-agent opportunities. Along with a partner, we purchased an agency and began calling specifically on network marketing companies. Within 11 months, we became the number-one agent for this long-distance reseller.

This experience gave me the opportunity to work with some of the top MLM companies along with their top people on the corporate and distributor sides of the business. Over the course of six years, I spoke at over 200 network marketing events and worked with the top-paid distributors in the industry.

All these experiences started with meeting Craig Tillotson while working on his home, and then five years later hearing that he was making $500,000 per month. Shortly after, I was working with distributors making $100,000 to $750,000 per month. I was flying on planes with them, joining them for road tours in their motorcoaches, and learning about the business and its possibilities.

This is about as positive an experience as anyone could ever hope for when getting involved with the MLM industry. As a result, I created a strong blueprint in my subconscious on the possibilities in MLM. In fact, my money blueprint with MLM as my primary business was set at about $500,000 per month. I was absolutely convinced I could and would make at least $500,000 per month in an MLM.

I was also working with owners and top executives on the corporate side of this business. Our largest client was doing about $700 million in sales, and they were in markets all over the world. Little did I know, not only was I creating a personal blueprint for income potential, I was also creating a blueprint for the possibilities of what my own MLM company could do someday. Several years later, I became the founder and CEO of my own MLM company. I'm often asked what my initial expectation was for my company. I have always said I truly believed my company was a billion-dollar household name in the making. At the time of this writing, we are well on our way to achieving this.

These MLM exposures turned out to be some of the greatest blessings of my life. They helped me establish a blueprint for success in MLM. I learned that my subconscious outlook on the possibilities of this business was immense. My outlook on the moneymaking possibilities was really high ($500,000 per month), and the emotions I experienced about that amount were all positive. In other words, the amount was also believable to my conscious thinking. Never once over the course of about 17 years did I ever

SUBCONSCIOUS
Things you
do not see

HABITS
BELIEFS
IMAGINATION

think $500,000 per month was wishful thinking. I truly believed it was a possibility. My subconscious was completely in alignment with my conscious and logical thinking on what I was capable of making in this business. So I went out and made it.

If you relate these experiences to the imprinting and layering process of a blueprint, you will see that my exposures throughout the years were placing positive imprints on my subconscious. My vibrant and positive imagination magnified those feel-good emotions, created strong beliefs, and formed supportive habits leading to success in the MLM profession. It's obvious that with this mindset, I would be attracting and manifesting positive information and experiences in my life.

The interesting thing is that, as of this writing, I have yet to make $500,000 in a single month in MLM, but I have made a tremendous amount of money through the years. I have enjoyed a lifestyle most people only dream of, and I attribute it to a strong MLM blueprint. The $500,000 month will happen, and then I will reset that blueprint to a higher level. Why? Because I know how to do it, and this book will show you how to do it as well.

But first, you must remember I was uniquely fortunate. Most people do not have these kinds of experiences with their MLM exposures—most people have the exact opposite experience. Think about it. The majority of people never make more than a couple hundred dollars per month in an MLM. Many never even earn the equivalent of their initial investment in commissions. As we know, human nature plays the blame game, and people blame everyone but themselves for their failure. With that blame game comes a lot of negative emotion.

Why was I uniquely fortunate? How is it possible that I had all these positive exposures when most people have negative ones?

Was it a stroke of fate that gave me the advantage over so many others? Well, it just so happens that I'm really not all that fond of the word fate. Destiny is a much better word. Fate carries with it the thought that what you manifest is out of your control. Destiny means you have control of what you manifest. Because of this, I went back and reflected again on all my exposures. Here is what I found.

EXPOSURE 1

My first exposure to MLM happened in 1978, when I was 14 years old. A friend and I were riding our BMX bikes through a subdivided neighborhood, and we started talking about someone who lived in that neighborhood who appeared to have a lot of money. My friend told me he heard the man was **on top of a money-pyramid thing** *where he made a percentage from the sales of thousands of people who were in the pyramid. He also heard we could join it, but he* **didn't know if it was legal or not**. *That's all I remember, but it must have registered subconsciously because I do remember the conversation, and that memory has surfaced many times in my life. It invoked an emotion of excitement around the* **possibility of making lots of money**.

Take a look at the first two phrases in bold:

On top of a money-pyramid thing
Didn't know if it was legal or not

From this exchange with my friend, it would have been possible for me to have had a completely different experience than I did. Think about it: There is some negative energy surrounding those two thoughts. I could have exposed my imagination to that negativity. If I had done that, every exposure thereafter may have become negative. Fortunately for me, I was a 14 year old with a wild imagination. I attached my thoughts to the third bolded phrase, the **possibility of making lots of money**. My imagination took over and subconsciously created the belief that MLM could make me lots of money. A feel-good emotion was generated, and I stored a positive memory around the possibilities of MLM. Because of that, my conscious thoughts around MLM were always positive, and I attracted information and experiences that supported that positivity.

An interesting note about this historical exposure: The friend I was riding bikes with focused on the negative thoughts of that conversation. While my imagination was exposed with "the possibility of making lots of money," his was exposed with "pyramid thing" and "didn't know if it was legal or not." Thirty-plus years later, I have experienced massive success in the MLM profession. He has refused to ever join one.

LET'S TAKE A LOOK AT EXPOSURE 2

My second exposure to MLM was when I was 22 years old, in the summer of 1986. I was home from college, working for my dad's company, earning money to go back for the fall semester. I went with one of my brothers to a job where we were finishing the basement of a large custom home in an affluent neighborhood. I remember being on a ladder, hanging a light fixture—something I did not enjoy doing. The owner of the home came through to check on things. He had some discussion with my brother and then left. I was blown away by how young this guy was. When he left, I asked my brother who he was and what he did for a living. My brother told me the homeowner's name was Craig Tillotson, and he did something with vitamins or skin care—my brother wasn't exactly sure what it was, but Craig made money selling these products. He also made money from the sales of those he recruited to sell the products. That was it. I don't remember my brother saying anything about it being an MLM or network marketing, but I do remember him saying we could join if we wanted.

Why is it that this experience excited me but had little or no effect on my brother? In fact, I remember him talking in a negative tone about Craig's work. As I look back now, I clearly see my subconscious was imprinted with positivity around MLM and the possibility of making lots of money. My thought pointed to positive imagination, and my subconscious triggered a memory and a feel-good emotion around the possibility of making lots of money.

If you go through all my exposures, you will see a similar trend. My thoughts were feeding my imagination and supporting a positive belief system around MLM. That is the very reason I kept getting exposed to positive MLM information and experiences.

As I help thousands of people in my workshops reflect on their life exposures to MLM, I find their thoughts are feeding their information and experiences (usually negative), they generate feel-bad emotions that imprint the subconscious, and their memory banks are loaded with negative stories. So they attract more of the same as they continue their journey. The majority of stories go something like this:

I first heard about an MLM from relatives or friends who ended up not having much success with the venture. Not only did they fail, but they also ended up with hurt feelings over the failure, and they now talk negatively about MLM in general. I then found an MLM I got excited about and attempted to build a business. I approached people I knew, liked, and respected, and received a negative pushback or flat-out rejection. I heard all their negative stories and experiences and was told to be very careful about spending too much time with an MLM.

These are highly common exposures that combine to form a negative MLM blueprint on the subconscious. Most of the time, those who are negatively impacted by these blueprints don't even know they have them. They get excited about an MLM opportunity. They attend some meetings and receive some powerful "how to" training. They are doing all the right things, but their subconscious has the blueprints for failure.

They write their warm-market list, cross people off that list before they ever attempt to call them, finally get the nerve to call someone, reluctantly give the invitation, and then wonder why their prospect didn't show up to the opportunity meeting. On occasion, they finally get someone to a meeting, they get them to see the presentation, and they reluctantly ask, "Would you like to join?" They are doing all the right things, but the reluctance is coming from their subconscious doubts and fears—and they are vibrating that energy to their prospect.

It's never what you say or do to prospects that will get them to join your MLM; to paraphrase the famous quote, it's how you make them *feel*. If they feel your reluctance, they usually will not join. So the new distributor, the one who is doing everything her upline asked her to do, still has a hard time getting people into the business. The distributor gets frustrated, creates another negative imprint, and adds to the negative blueprint she has about MLM.

The simple fact of the matter is that most people don't usually allow their imagination to intervene in a positive way. Most people focus their thoughts solely on the negative information and experiences they have, and they live in fear. Then they wonder why things are not working out for them.

The other thing we find is that people get started in MLM with all the right intentions. They even get exposed to excellent personal development training. That training starts them on the right track, but their daily negative exposures intervene. This happens for two reasons: 1) There is so much negative in the conscious world about MLM, it creeps in on a regular basis, and 2) there's a pretty good chance they've got deeply embedded negative MLM imprints in their subconscious.

So how do we turn this around? Every plan for positive change begins with a knowledge and awareness of where we are. In fact, awareness is usually half the equation for change. We must first gain an awareness of where we are with our current MLM blueprint, discover what kind of imprints have been placed on our subconscious over time, and see if those imprints are in alignment with our desires. To figure this out, we need to start by exploring the exposures we have had to MLM.

CHAPTER 3

Exploration

Through the process of creating the *MLM Blueprint Workshop*, I have discovered some shortcuts that can really help you get to the core of your blueprint issues. Five current (ongoing) MLM exposures are common to most people attempting to build an MLM business. There are also six significant historical (past) MLM exposures most people have had that need to be analyzed. Each of these exposures, whether current or historical, has a dramatic impact on your current MLM blueprint and on the blueprint you are creating on an ongoing basis.

CURRENT (ONGOING)-EXPOSURES CHECKLIST

1) What others think and feel about MLM
2) What you think and feel about MLM
3) What you choose to expose yourself to about MLM
4) The three shutdowns in MLM:
   - When your prospect shuts you down
   - When your new team member shuts down
   - When duplication on your team shuts down
5) The three rise-aboves in MLM:
   - When people rise and cheer for you
   - When you rise and cheer for your people
   - When your check rises and you cheer

The list of "ongoing exposures" is just that: ongoing. You experience these in some form every day of your active MLM career. You will learn to analyze your MLM experiences based on this list, and it will dramatically help you keep things in a positive perspective. Your ongoing exposures serve as a checklist for taking control of what is being imprinted on your subconscious.

This checklist will also help you analyze and correct your historical exposures. Most people have major blocks caused by historical exposures that created a weak MLM blueprint on their subconscious, and this prevents them from succeeding in this profession.

SIGNIFICANT HISTORICAL EXPOSURES FOR YOU TO ANALYZE:

1) Your first exposure—the first time you can remember hearing about the concept of MLM
2) Exposures where other people affected you, positively or negatively
3) Exposure that sold you on the MLM concept
4) Exposure that created a money blueprint for MLM, where you established a belief as to how much money you could make
5) When you first joined an MLM and what your experience was
6) Exposures that shut you down and exposures that helped you rise above

As you explore each of these historical exposures, analyze each using the Current (Ongoing)-Exposures Checklist on the first page of this chapter to see which type of ongoing exposure affected it. Using this process, you'll find what your blueprint issues might be, and you'll also discover how you can fix or strengthen them. For an example, we'll analyze my significant historical exposures using the ongoing-exposure checklist.

My first exposure to MLM:

I was 14 years old, and heard about a money pyramid where a new neighbor was making lots of money. I remember getting excited about the possibilities of making lots of money. A few years later, I was working on the family electrical business on a custom home, owned by a young guy who was making lots of money in an MLM. This triggered a feel-good memory from my first exposure and once again tapped my imagination on its possibilities. As I check to see the types of ongoing exposures used here, I discover how I created a strong and positive blueprint.

Using the ongoing-exposure checklist for analysis: I was affected by what I thought and felt about MLM, and I didn't care what my friend thought or felt about MLM. My thoughts were positive; his were negative. I chose to focus on "the possibilities of making lots of money" rather than "this being a pyramid thing." The shutdowns and rise-above exposures did not apply (they typically don't with your first exposure).

Using the ongoing-exposure checklist for analysis: Exposures where other people affected me (positive or negative): My first invitation to join an MLM came from my older brother Kris, who was very excited by the possibilities offered in an MLM that sold insurance services. This was one of the last memories I had of my brother before I moved away from home. A few months later, he passed away.

Using the ongoing-exposure checklist for analysis: Fortunately for me, my brother's thoughts and feelings about MLM were positive—so were mine. We both chose to expose ourselves to the positive aspects of MLM. The shutdowns and rise-above exposures did not apply.

Exposure that sold me on the concept of MLM:

This was my second invitation to join an MLM, where a high-profile leader taught me about leverage and the power of duplication. He also made reference to the number-one income earner, who was the same man referred to in my second exposure.

Using the ongoing-exposure checklist for analysis: What I thought and felt about MLM was already positive. My thoughts supported the positive information the presenter was giving me in this story. I was exposing myself to positivity by being at this meeting. Shutdowns and rise-aboves did not apply in this story.

Exposure that created my money blueprint for MLM:

In my case, this historical exposure was the same one as the exposure that sold me on the concept of MLM mentioned above.

Using the ongoing-exposure checklist for analysis: What I thought and felt about the money possibilities became my dominant exposure. Even though others around me were cynical about those possibilities, my beliefs were in place, and I laughed off the cynics. I knew it was possible to make over $500,000 per month in MLM because I had an example of it in my memory. From that point on, I exposed myself to people and stories of people making that kind of money in MLM. I was attracting those people in my life. The shutdowns and rise-aboves did not apply in this example.

My experience when first joining an MLM:

I joined my first MLM and immediately began creating support materials to help myself and others present the products and opportunity. I was able to hang out and work with top-producing distributors of that company.

Using the ongoing-exposure checklist for analysis: Now I was in an environment where what I thought and felt about MLM (positive) was in perfect alignment with what others thought and felt about MLM (positive). In that environment, I was exposing myself to a plethora of positive information about MLMs. No shutdowns yet, but the rise-aboves were beginning to happen. People were rising up and cheering for me, and the numbers on my paychecks were getting bigger. This is unique because most people experience shutdowns before they experience rise-above exposures.

My shutdown and rise-above exposures:

I made my warm-market list and contacted my first prospect, a friend who had previously invited me to the meeting that led to me joining the MLM Neways. My friend joined me in the business. I began contacting others on my warm market list. They were family members and friends of the family. These were people I highly respected and was excited to sponsor in the business. I started getting shutdowns. I started hearing the negatives of MLM from these people. They questioned my wisdom and made a point to set me straight on what I was getting into. I was not prepared for this. To this point, I had been spoiled with positive exposures.

Using the ongoing-exposure checklist for analysis: For the first time, I was allowing negative thoughts and feelings of other people to pull me down. I was allowing negative exposures of MLM to enter my mind, and I experienced shutdown number one as others close to me were shutting me down. Those I had sponsored on my team were also beginning to shut down. My first sponsor and I committed six hours of our Saturdays to building the business. He quit that commitment on the third Saturday.

I must admit that my examples may not be the best ones because they were typically far more positive than most. I did not even get a negative until we got to my shutdowns. Most people will be dealing with negatives throughout each of their historical exposures. The cool thing about this process is you can easily discover the strengths and weaknesses of your MLM blueprint and you can see exactly how to fix them. The fixes are found in how you utilize the ongoing exposures.

At one of our *MLM Blueprint Workshops*, I had a student who wrote down his historical exposures and used the checklist to explore them. His example represents a more typical experience, so you may be able to better relate to this example because he dealt with negatives from the beginning.

His first exposure to MLM:

David worked with his older brother in the construction business. Construction was all he knew. In his mind, it was the only way for him to make money and support his family. David's older brother invited him to a meeting where he met a slick salesman who used all kinds of high-pressure tactics to tell him why he needed to pay a bunch of money and get involved with their business deal, an MLM. It was a bad experience for David, and he was turned off from the beginning.

Using the ongoing-exposure checklist for analysis: In David's case, what others thought and felt about MLM was positive. However, their approach (flashy high pressure) turned their positive into his negative. What David thought and felt was negative and became his dominant emotion. He began to expose himself to other people who also had bad experiences with the MLM craze. With those people, he would swap stories about how crazy MLM people were. Shutdowns and rise-aboves did not apply.

Exposures where other people affected him (positive or negative):

David used his first-time exposure again here as it had a profound, negative effect on him.

Exposure that sold him on the concept of MLM:

David remembers sitting down with two guys who showed him, on a piece of paper, the concept of leverage and duplication. At the time, life was good for him, and his confidence level was high. Because of this, things clicked for him. He got excited and believed he could give MLM another shot.

Using the ongoing-exposure checklist for analysis: What others thought and felt was positive and, because David was receptive, their positivity along with their professional non-pressure approach impressed him and transformed his thoughts. They referred David to positive reinforcement (books and tapes) about the profession, and he began to expose himself to this positive material. Shutdowns and rise-aboves did not apply here.

Exposure that created a money blueprint for MLM:

This came from the same exposure that sold David on the concept of MLM. One of men presenting was making about $6,000 per month. David instantly believed he could do the same, and the prospect excited him.

Using the ongoing-exposure checklist for analysis: Others thought—and told David—that anyone could make $6,000 or more per month, part-time, in this business; one man, his presenter, was already making that and was just getting started. So David started believing that $6,000 per month was obtainable, and he was excited. Because he was around these folks, David was introduced to others who had these same beliefs. He was exposed to books, audio, speeches, and stories where people from all walks of life were achieving their financial goals.

His experience when first joining an MLM:

David joined the opportunity that he was presented and immediately sponsored two distributors into his new business. He remembers going to an event with his wife—and he had not yet told her about joining the business. (Note: This is probably not a good idea.) Unbeknownst to him, when they got to the meeting, David was called up on stage and recognized for getting his first two distributors. His wife was not happy. In fact, due to her own negative exposures to MLM, she was livid. Her negativity immediately shut him down. To make matters worse, several days after that meeting, some of his upline sponsors showed up at their home when his wife was home alone. They pressured her to order several things out of a catalog so that a volume requirement could be met. When David found out, it upset him because it put his wife over the edge. After that, she would have nothing to do with the business, and he followed suit.

Using the ongoing-exposure checklist for analysis: What David's wife thought and felt had a stronger impact than what David thought and felt about MLM. His blueprint was not strong enough to keep him in the business. Because there was so much negativity from his family and his wife's family, they both immediately exposed themselves to the MLM negativity once again. David's wife became one of his significant others that shut him down.

His shutdown and rise-above exposures:

David joined the business, immediately sponsored two distributors, and the group rose up and cheered for him. He remembered how good that felt, at least until he got back to his seat where his unhappy wife was waiting for him. In presenting this opportunity to others close to him, he experienced some dramatic shutdowns he was not prepared for. The same older brother mentioned in his first-time exposure let David know they were construction workers and that he would fail at trying to make money any other way. Wow! Other family members, including his father, had similar responses when he approached them. Those shutdowns, along with the experience with his wife, were devastating. David was not prepared, and what others thought and felt was far more important than what he thought and felt. He chose to expose himself to their negativity and to negative information they had heard about MLM. He was not prepared for the shutdowns. Even though he did have a wonderful rise-above experience, the shutdowns were far bigger, and he was completely blindsided by them.

What the *MLM Blueprint Workshop* did for this man, and thousands of people like him, was to help him explore his historical exposures. In doing so, he discovered what his mental and emotional blocks were. By using the ongoing exposure checklist, he was able to see how he forfeited control of the life he desired to live.

The ongoing-exposure checklist helped him understand this:

- What **you** think and feel is what matters.
- What others think and feel matters **only** if it's in alignment with your MLM positivity.
- It's not what you are exposed to that matters; it's what you choose to expose yourself to that matters.
- Being prepared for shutdowns is the most important way to protect yourself as you create a healthy MLM blueprint.
- Rise-above exposures become your goal and they become your focus. With them as your focus, they begin to manifest. Rise-above exposures are the greatest antidote to shutdown exposures.

WHERE DO YOU GO FROM HERE

In our *MLM Blueprint Workshops*, we lead people through a simple discovery process to help them recall their historical exposures. We then summarize their historical exposures and check them against the list of ongoing exposures, as I just did in this chapter. This is a powerful exploration and discovery process. You can do the same thing by following the example of this chapter and going through the same process as outlined in the next.

CHAPTER 4

Discovery

In the last two chapters we analyzed a detailed history of my MLM exposures. Your goal is to create the same detailed written history of all your exposures. Initially, you may not remember offhand the kind of detail you see in mine. But it is important to recall as much detail as possible from all your exposures. To help you do this, I have developed a list of questions that will help trigger memories. In our workshop format, we take our participants through a series of exercises where these questions are asked; participants are coached through the process and given a chance to share their answers and ask questions along the way.

Shortly after the phone call where I held my very first—and very spontaneous—blueprint-coaching session, I was asked to give an unexpected speech at a Friday-night distributor event, which also led to my first opportunity to test my questions with another coaching participant. Because the MLM blueprint concept was fresh on my mind, I used it as the basis of my presentation. As I began my "shoot from the hip" speech, I enthusiastically shared my experience on the phone call and introduced a group of 200-plus distributors to the concept of MLM blueprints and how they dramatically affect your ability to succeed. I mentioned that if you are hitting a wall in your business-building efforts, chances are good that you have an experience or an exposure imprinted on your subconscious that is preventing you from progressing to the next level.

This simple idea struck a chord with many of the distributors at that meeting.

One of our rising stars, Linda, came up to me after the event and asked if I would be willing to coach her. She said my blueprint speech had a significant impact on her. She had heard of a money blueprint but never an MLM blueprint, and hearing about one had created an "aha moment" for her. In fact, as Linda said those words, she began to cry. She said she was absolutely convinced she must have had an experience that was dramatically holding her back, but she had no idea what it was. She believed my coaching would help her trigger the memory so she could deal with it. I told her I would be honored to coach her and that I would be taking her through a series of questions to help find answers. We set up a time for a phone call.

As I walked away from that conversation, I was thinking, *Oh great, what questions am I going to ask? How can I possibly help her trigger a memory she was obviously trying to suppress?* I was no psychologist, even though I wanted to be one at one time in my life. I guess now I would have my chance. I heard a speaker say one time, "Fake it until you make it," and at this moment, I decided to follow that advice.

As I began my first call with Linda, I was upfront and honest. I told her I wasn't sure what the best approach would be, so I started asking what appeared to be the obvious questions:

- What was your first experience with MLM?
- Who introduced you?
- What is the person who first introduced you saying today about MLM?

- Do you personally know someone who is highly successful in an MLM?
- Does your husband support you in your MLM business? (I already knew that he did.)

After asking several questions like this, it appeared she had fairly decent exposures to the industry. Not knowing what to do, I simply kept asking questions. I had no idea where the answers were taking us, but we just kept going.

I finally asked her to tell me who, other than her husband, was she closest to and whose opinion did she respect the most? Linda gave me the same answer to both questions. It was her twin sister. They had been very close their entire lives. Her sister worked in a professional-sales position for a large corporation, and she was very successful. I asked Linda what her sister thought about MLM. She said her twin did not like MLM and shared the following story.

At the beginning of her network marketing career, Linda and her entire extended family—parents, siblings, and children—were all out at dinner. Everyone was talking about work. When Linda began talking about her MLM business, however, her sister said, "If you are going to talk about that, we are not staying."

Linda answered, "Everyone else talks about their work; I should be able to as well." As the conversation continued about her MLM, her sister, sister's husband, and their children abruptly got up from the table and left the restaurant. As Linda was saying this, she stopped herself and said, "That's it. That is my block. I need validation from my sister that my MLM business is OK."

"I'm glad you feel like you found your block, but I have a few more questions," I said, knowing we were getting somewhere important. "Do you really need validation from your sister that your MLM business is OK?"

Linda said, "No, but I want her respect."

"Are you even sure that your sister hates MLM as much as you think she does?" I asked.

"I'm pretty sure she does," Linda answered.

I told her we could not continue our coaching session until she met with her sister. I encouraged her to have a candid but loving conversation and to confront her sister about the time she abruptly left dinner when they were talking about Linda's business. Most importantly, regardless of whatever reservations her sister had about the business, I asked Linda to tell her sister that she loved her MLM business, that it was a big part of who she was as a person, and to let her sister know she doesn't have to like or approve of the business, but she does need to respect that Linda absolutely loves what she does.

We ended that call, and Linda did meet with her sister. She immediately called me after they had met, so excited to report the conversation they'd had. What Linda really found out is that her sister respects her and the fact that she does something different but said she could never do it herself because she felt Linda's income was dependent on too many people.

First, Linda said she was shocked that her sister barely recalled the incident at the restaurant. All that time, it had blocked Linda's development and bothered her so much, and it wasn't even on her sister's radar. The second and most important lesson she learned was that as much as her sister didn't like MLM, that feeling was equal in strength to how much Linda did not like the traditional 8-to-5 corporate scene. She had her sister's respect, but they agreed to disagree on their career choices. Linda was then able to let go of this limiting, negative thought and fully engage in her business.

After telling me this, she said, "Can you believe it?"

"Well, yes, actually I can," I said. "I can believe it because, first of all, you are a dynamic individual, and I can only imagine how your twin sister must feel about you. Second of all, we as human beings have a tendency to make things up in our minds, especially when we are seeking validation from others."

We continued with a few additional coaching calls, and I was able to formulate a list of questions and exercises that exposed the MLM imprints in her subconscious. I was also able to work with her on how she could make dramatic improvements to those imprints and re-create an MLM blueprint for success. After completing these sessions, Linda quickly advanced to a prestigious level in our company, and has gone on to be one of our best trainers and fastest team-builders in the company.

After those calls, I worked these questions and exercises into a workbook and conducted several more *MLM Blueprint Workshops*. The most effective way to learn and apply the blueprinting principles is to attend an interactive event. By being with a group of like-minded network marketers, you can take advantage of a certified trainer who will facilitate discussion of the group. Information at the back of this book will explain how you can find and register for one of these events. In the meantime, we can take you through that process in this book, and you can walk yourself through these exercises by answering the questions as best you can here.

DISCOVERING YOUR CURRENT MLM BLUEPRINT

The first thing you want to do in the discovery process is to recall your historical exposures to MLM (for examples you can refer back to my historical exposures in Chapter 3). By answering the following questions, you will refresh your memory so that you can recall your significant exposures and record them precisely.

1) When approaching people with your MLM opportunity, what is your first emotion when you hear the question "Is this an MLM?"

_____
_____
_____
_____
_____

2) Would you rather approach people you know or people you don't know about your MLM? Why?

_____
_____
_____
_____
_____

3) What are the people around you saying about MLM today? How does it affect you?

_____
_____
_____
_____
_____

4) Did your impression of MLM change after the first time you approached your family or friends about an MLM? Why?

_____
_____
_____
_____
_____

5) If you have sponsored people who have quit the business, did your impression of MLM change after they quit? Why?

_____

_____

_____

_____

_____

6) If you have experienced a downline that stopped growing or duplicating, did your impression of MLM change? Why?

_____

_____

_____

_____

_____

7) What is the highest amount of monthly income made by any person who has sponsored you in an MLM?

_____

8) What is the highest amount of monthly income ever made in an MLM by someone you personally know?

_____

9) What is the amount of monthly income you truly believe you can make in an MLM? Why?

_____

_____

_____

_____

_____

Use the answers to these questions to help you write your significant historical exposures on the next few pages. You may look back at mine in the previous chapter for reference. Analyze your historical exposures using the ongoing-exposure checklist.

Your first exposure to the concept of MLM:

_____

_____

_____

_____

_____

_____

_____

_____

_____

_____

_____

_____

_____

_____

_____

Ongoing-exposure checklist (analyze only those that apply)
- What you think and feel about MLM
- What others think and feel about MLM
- What you choose to expose yourself to about MLM
- Shutdowns
- Rise-aboves

_____

_____

_____

_____

_____

_____

_____

_____

_____

_____

Exposure where others affected you in a positive or negative way:

_____

_____

_____

_____

_____

_____

_____

_____

_____

_____

_____

_____

_____

_____

Ongoing-exposure checklist (analyze only those that apply)
- What you think and feel about MLM
- What others think and feel about MLM
- What you choose to expose yourself to about MLM
- Shutdowns
- Rise-aboves

_____

_____

_____

_____

_____

_____

_____

_____

_____

_____

Exposure that sold you on the concept of MLM:

_____

_____

_____

_____

_____

_____

_____

_____

_____

_____

_____

_____

_____

_____

Ongoing-exposure checklist (analyze only those that apply)
- What you think and feel about MLM
- What others think and feel about MLM
- What you choose to expose yourself to about MLM
- Shutdowns
- Rise-aboves

_____

_____

_____

_____

_____

_____

_____

_____

_____

_____

Exposure that created your money blueprint for MLM:

_____
_____
_____
_____
_____
_____
_____
_____
_____
_____
_____
_____
_____
_____
_____
_____
_____

Ongoing-exposure checklist (analyze only those that apply)
- What you think and feel about MLM
- What others think and feel about MLM
- What you choose to expose yourself to about MLM
- Shutdowns
- Rise-aboves

_____
_____
_____
_____
_____
_____
_____
_____
_____
_____

Your experience when first joining an MLM:

_____

_____

_____

_____

_____

_____

_____

_____

_____

_____

_____

_____

_____

_____

_____

Ongoing-exposure checklist (analyze only those that apply)
- What you think and feel about MLM
- What others think and feel about MLM
- What you choose to expose yourself to about MLM
- Shutdowns
- Rise-aboves

_____

_____

_____

_____

_____

_____

_____

_____

_____

_____

Your shutdown and rise-above exposures:

_____

_____

_____

_____

_____

_____

_____

_____

_____

_____

_____

_____

_____

Ongoing-exposure checklist (analyze only those that apply)
- What you think and feel about MLM
- What others think and feel about MLM
- What you choose to expose yourself to about MLM
- Shutdowns
- Rise-aboves

_____

_____

_____

_____

_____

_____

_____

_____

_____

I really hope you took the time to go through this exercise. If you did, you are going to discover some amazing things about how you currently think and feel about your MLM business. You will also find that most people's attitudes and opinions about MLM are based on non-factual or emotional experiences. Those could be their own experiences or from people they know and love.

It is a known fact that the vast majority of what people are exposed to on a daily basis is negative. That is exactly the same when you analyze people's exposure to MLM. What's interesting is that people who are successful in MLM choose to ignore the negativity and focus on the positive. That is why they are successful. Yet most people who look into and even get involved with an MLM allow the negativity to dictate what is imprinted on the subconscious. They allow other people's negativity to determine their outlook, their story, and, ultimately, their MLM blueprint.

The next chapters are going to show you a simple but powerful process on how to re-create an MLM blueprint for massive success. Remember, the subconscious manifests your reality. If we can get the MLM blueprint of your subconscious in alignment with the conscious action steps and plans provided by your company's leaders, you will be on your way to earning the residual income of your dreams.

CHAPTER 5

Take Control:
Create an MLM Blueprint
for Massive Success

Thoughts are created from the information and experiences in our conscious world. Those thoughts create exposures on the imagination where they are magnified, and beliefs and habits form from there.

If you want to strengthen your MLM blueprint, you need exposures with positive and factual information about the strengths of MLM, and you need quality experiences. You must also use your imagination to create new affirmations or "I am" statements you can use to nourish your subconscious. This chapter covers some powerful activities that will help you cleanse your blueprint and create more consistent blueprinting for building a successful network marketing business.

It's astonishing that we will take at face value what others say about MLM and use that information as an exposure to the subconscious. Most of the time, people who have a negative opinion about the industry know very little about it. And what they do know, they typically learned from someone else who knows very little about it. Because of this, there is a lot of negative and inaccurate information out there.

It's also astonishing how much value people put on what others think. This is one of the biggest showstoppers for people getting into an MLM. They simply care way too much about what other people think. Instead of allowing their own mind and heart to guide their attitudes and actions, they allow someone else's cynical, uneducated attitudes to guide them on the continual pathway of mediocrity.

It is time for new information and positive nourishment. It is time to listen to your own heart and live out the genius that is in you. If you have been attracted to an MLM opportunity and want to be a success, *there is a reason!* Your heart, your mind, and your genius guided you there. Stand up and think for yourself.

You have already learned there are five ongoing MLM exposures, and they play a significant role in the strength of your MLM blueprint. Take control of those ongoing exposures. Cleanse them. Nourish them with positivity. Strengthen them with facts about human behavior, information about MLM's capacity to help you acquire wealth, statements of affirmation that nourish your imagination, and personal development plans that will produce positive results. Here is a simple example of this cleansing and strengthening process.

ONGOING EXPOSURES 1 AND 2

What others think and feel, and what you think and feel.

Cleanse, nourish, and strengthen the effects these two things have on you. You can do this with an exposure to these cleansing and strengthening facts:

- **Fact #1:** Personal success is never determined by what someone else thinks, especially someone who knows very little about what excites you.
- **Fact #2:** Personal success is always determined by what you think and how you feel about what excites you.
- **Fact #3:** You attract what you think and feel. You can choose to think and feel for yourself, or you can allow others to think and feel for you.
- **Fact #4:** Those who have a strong MLM blueprint rarely if ever hear the negative from others. Why? They attract what they think and feel. They attract others who are excited to join them in their business.
- **Fact #5:** You can follow a blueprint created from past failures and cynical thinking, or you can follow a blueprint created by your excitement, your desires, and the examples of successful people around you.
- **Fact #6:** Ninety percent of the population works as employees. That's all they've known and that's what they have been trained to believe is good and normal. Only 10 percent own their own business, according to the Kaufmann Foundation Study on Entrepreneurial Activity. It's that same 90 percent who are giving you their opinions about MLM. Do you *really* think *they* are qualified to direct your future?

ONGOING EXPOSURE 3:

What you choose to expose yourself to.

Let's start with accurate information about the MLM profession. When we talk about network marketing, we are not talking about some rogue, unproven profession. Many popular and classic thought leaders, including Jim Rohn and Robert Kiyosaki, have shared valuable information about this profession.

According to the 2009 research done by the Direct Selling Association, the MLM industry is over 100 years old and a $28.33 billion industry in the United States alone. Globally, the statistic is much higher: MLM is an approximately $114 billion global profession involving about 65 million people. Compare that to these well-known industries: The NFL is a $9 billion industry, the worldwide music industry revenues for 2010 were $66.4 billion, and the global movies and entertainment market generated total revenues of $109.4 billion in 2009.

Word-of-mouth marketing creates a spectacular platform. Think about the growth of social networking. Do you know anyone who isn't involved in some way? Facebook in particular has created a platform where messages, positive and negative, are broadcast instantaneously among millions of people every minute. If you like something you see, you may repost it and share it you're your friends, who will share it with theirs—and on and on. In network marketing, people tell their friends about a product or opportunity, and that interaction makes them care about your brand, which in turn makes your business grow.

More and more, consumers are deciding what to buy according to word-of-mouth messaging, including network marketing, direct sales, and referral marketing. Several well-known companies are joining the direct sales world, including Remington, Unilever, L'Oreal, and Mars. After purchasing a network marketing company, billionaire Warren Buffett said it was the best investment he'd ever made, according to *Entrepreneur* magazine. Bestselling author Tom Peters, who wrote *In Search of Excellence*, calls network marketing the first truly revolutionary shift in marketing in the last 50 years.

The global research and consultant company McKenzie reports that already 67 percent of consumer decisions are driven by word of mouth, and 90 percent of customers identify word of mouth as the best, most reliable, and trustworthy source for product information, according to research group NOP World. This is compared to 14 percent trust for advertisers, and even less trust for celebrities, at just 8 percent. This is why there is a massive shift toward word of mouth, referral marketing, network marketing, and direct sales.

In fact, in an age of massive commercial-marketing competition and clutter, word-of-mouth or referral marketing is being considered the most effective and powerful form of marketing. The average consumer receives thousands of commercial messages per day. Also, marketing costs three times as much now for half the results versus just 20 years ago. All the trends point toward direct sales or the MLM industry as a thriving solution to selling products and creating wealth.

I have gained my own perspective about the value of MLM. People generate income in four primary categories:

- Employee
- Employer
- Investor
- Entertainer

The employee: Has severe limits to what they can make and little or no control over their time, freedom, or future. There was a time when security was a benefit to being an employee, but those times appear to be over.

The employer: Deals with enormous start-up costs, regulations, workers compensation, inventories, employee management, cash-flow issues, and must plan for recession cycles.

The investor: Deals with many moving elements outside of their control. Economic cycles can be highly lucrative and highly devastating, and the shifts change rapidly.

The entertainer: Those who actually earn a living as entertainers are a small and select group. They include musicians, actors, athletes, writers, and more. Royalties, endorsements, and contracts can be highly lucrative—and don't we all wish we were in this category?

The general public is usually under-funded to become an employer, under-educated and under-capitalized to become an investor, and under-talented or under-connected to become an entertainer. That leaves the general public (90 percent) in the employee category. As of this writing, unemployment is at 8.3 percent, so this category has even more challenges.

Ironically, I am writing this gloomy data one day after listening to a Las Vegas cab driver give me his "state of the economy" speech during a 20-minute ride from the airport to my hotel. I'm sure I don't need to explain how painful that cab ride was. There are two reasons why it was painful. First, I despise negative talk. And second, I ached for this cab driver. I ached for him because he represents the 90 percent who are watching the news every night and buying into the gloom and doom. I ache for that 90 percent because they are the ones who attack the MLM blueprints of those striving to make something better for themselves.

My perspective on the value of MLM is simple: MLM or network marketing is a solution to all the challenges I just mentioned. In fact, it is the only solution for the general public or the masses, and this is why: MLM gives me the opportunity to be self-employed, with low start-up costs, no employees, no overhead, and very little risk. It gives me a system to follow, and connects me to an upline of people who want me to succeed. There is no limit as to what I can make. It will give to me what I put into it. Network marketing moves an individual out of the employee category. It keeps that individual from dealing with employer or investor issues. And, most importantly, it gives that individual the opportunity to make top-level entertainer's money. There is no other opportunity in existence that can do that.

When you are armed with this kind of information, it is a lot easier to allow someone's cynical, uneducated opinion about MLM to roll right off you. This kind of information will strengthen your blueprint over time. It will help you dissolve any reluctance in your vibrations or your voice when you approach someone about your MLM opportunity.

EXTRAORDINARY EXPERIENCES

In addition to information exposures, you can choose to expose yourself to extraordinary experiences in this profession. My early exposures were positive experiences. I went to excellent meetings, worked with top-level distributors, listened to positive audios, and cultivated other positive exposures. Your MLM company and your upline provide you with countless experiences. In my company, we call it "staying connected." You have access to conference calls, opportunity meetings, training events, regional conferences, incentive trips, and national conventions. By staying connected with what your company and upline provide, you gain control of your experiences. They become increasingly positive, they validate your positive outlook, and they strengthen your MLM blueprint.

I recall an experience I had with the top two income-earners in my company. We had just spent the past five days touring the major cities of Australia. We concluded the tour by having a big training event near Sydney. After we finished the event, the three of us were walking around an exciting little beach town called Coogee Beach. It was in late February, so it was winter back home in Utah but summertime in Australia. We found a nice place to have dinner, bask in the evening sun, and watch all the people buzzing around. One of the guys made a comment that will stick with me forever and created yet another positive imprint on my MLM blueprint. He said, "What other kind of business allows you to be on the other side of the world with some of your dearest friends creating memories like this?" That is what this business is all about. There is adventure in every day. Life was meant to be lived with passion, and MLM provides us with ongoing positive and adventurous experiences.

ONGOING EXPOSURE #4

Being prepared for the shutdowns.

There are three primary shutdown exposures in this business:
1) When your prospect shuts you down
2) When your new team member shuts down
3) When duplication on your team shuts down

Most of the time, people in this profession are unprepared for these shutdowns. This can be devastating to their MLM business. It can also damage their MLM blueprint. If you can be proactive toward the emotional experience of these shutdowns, you can quickly regain control and even use that control to strengthen your blueprint.

Shutdown #1: When your prospect shuts you down. You approach someone you know and care about, and you are convinced they are perfect for the business. Together, you will do amazing things, and both of you will enjoy success together. You excitedly give her the invitation. She shuts you down. Not only does she shut you down, but she proceeds to tell you how crazy you are and that she can't believe you would approach her about something like an MLM.

This is a common experience. It usually happens to someone who is new to the business—and completely unprepared for it. The typical emotional experience is nothing short of being mortified. If you are caught off guard with this kind of shutdown, it can be devastating.

How do you handle it?

1) Recognize it as a shutdown and know it is a common experience.

2) Know the shutdown is not personal. It's about her, not about you. She is either not ready, or she has fears about what you introduced. Your job is not to try to figure her out. Your job is to accept her answer and move on.

3) Understand you are playing the law of averages. Use the acronym: SW, SW, SW, Next (Some will, some won't, so what? Next!). The more times you share your opportunity, the better you will be able to play the law of averages.

4) It's OK to feel a brief emotional letdown, but keep it brief and move on. Remember it's not what happens to you; it's what you allow yourself to think and feel about what happens to you. Simply move on.

5) Understand it may not be easy to take this advice, but practice makes perfect.

I have found that by simply being aware that these shutdowns happen, you will be more prepared and will get over them much more quickly.

Shutdown #2: The new distributor on your team who shuts down. You sign up a new distributor on your team. He is excited and makes commitments to follow your daily business-building system. You are excited to follow up with him to see how he is doing, but you find he has done nothing. You are patient and call him several times to see if he is ready to start. He is not. He ends up not returning your calls. This can be devastating because you finally got someone to sign up. It appeared he was going to be as committed as you, and now, you would enjoy some duplication. And then it doesn't happen.

How do you handle it?

1) Recognize it as a shutdown, and remember the simple law of averages. Most people who make big money in MLM can attribute the majority of their income to three or four legs in their organization. I have heard seasoned distributors report they have personally enrolled 100-plus people into the business over several years, which duplicated to a team of thousands, sometimes hundreds of thousands of people. The majority of those people come from three or four legs. This is really good to know because when one

quits, you will know it's the law of averages at work in your business.

2) Know that it's not personal. It's about them, not about you. They are either not ready, or they have had life get in the way. It happens. Your job is not to try to figure them out. Your job is to accept that they are not ready and move on. The greatest advice I have heard about this comes from the top income-earner in my company. He says he never chases anybody on his team. He lets them do the chasing. If they call you, and they show up on the conference calls, and they attend the meetings, they are ready and you can now go and work with them. If you chase them, it sets you up for this kind of shutdown.

3) Use the acronym: SW, SW, SW, Next (Some will, some won't, so what? Next!).

4) It's OK to feel a brief emotional letdown, but keep it brief and move on. Remember it's not what happens to you; it's what you allow yourself to think and feel about what happens to you. Simply move on.

5) Understand it may not be easy to take this advice, but practice makes perfect.

Shutdown #3: The duplication on your team that shuts down. This happens to distributors who are a little further along in building a team. They have advanced several levels in the pay plan, they have several hundred or a few thousand people in their downline, and they are used to checking their back office and seeing several people added to their team each day. All of a sudden, it appears that the duplication stops. Their team growth hits the skids. They can't figure out what is happening.

How to handle it?

1) Recognize this as a shutdown, and it is part of the business most everyone experiences.

2) Always remember people do what you do, not what you say. If you need your team members to sponsor people, then you need to sponsor people. If you see your duplication slowing down, simply work the law of averages and sponsor more people. Activity motivates people more than anything else. If your team sees activity by you or new people you are sponsoring, they will feel the buzz and re-activate.

3) Time to get controversial: The solution to this issue is not to hold more training meetings. You read me right. Having a series of training meetings will not solve this problem. If you want your team to start growing again, you need to do exactly what you need your team to do. Don't get me wrong. There is a time and a place for training meetings. They should be part of a consistent training program held by your company and/or upline support. You might be that upline support. Be consistent with your training plan. Never add trainings when your duplication slows down.

If you are prepared for the shutdown experiences, you will do your MLM blueprint a world of good. Remember it is never the shutdown that hurts you; it's how you choose to respond to the shutdown that will have a negative or positive effect on your ongoing MLM blueprint. The choice is yours.

Another thing that will dramatically help you take control of shutdowns is to focus on your activities, not on the outcome of your activities. If you focus on the outcome of your activities, you will be disappointed. If you focus on the activities and trust the law of averages, you can detach yourself from the outcome. This is a huge shift. It is one of the biggest keys to success in this business. Focus on the activities and allow the outcome to happen when it happens.

ONGOING EXPOSURE #5

Manifesting the rise-above experiences

As mentioned before, the greatest antidote for the shutdown experiences are the rise-above experiences.

Let's remind you of what they are:
1) When others rise and cheer for you
2) When you rise and cheer for your people
3) When your check rises and you cheer

Network marketing is the greatest recognition profession in the world. When you get started with your company, achieve their first benchmark or goal as fast as you can. Regardless of whether you think you need this or not, you need to be recognized for accomplishment. Hit those goals and allow others to rise and cheer for you. I like to associate this with playing golf. The reason most people continue to golf is because of the one or two perfect shots they made out of the 100-plus shots they took during an 18-hole game. (You can tell what kind of golfer I am by saying 100-plus shots—emphasis on the "plus.")

In your MLM business, the shutdowns are all those frustrating or imperfect shots. The rise-above experiences are the one or two perfect shots that keep you going in the game. The more you play, the more rise-above (or perfect) shots you have. Great golfers have far more than one or two perfect shots in an 18-hole game.

Those who are experienced and become professional network marketers have far more than one or two rise-above experiences in the months and years they are active in their businesses.

Surprising to the novice in this business, the "rise and cheer" for your team members has far more impact than having others rise and cheer for you. You want to help those you sponsor get recognized as quickly as possible.

Having your checks get bigger is always an exhilarating experience. The best way to make this happen in any compensation plan is to help your team members grow their own checks. These are the things we should always focus on.

SUMMARY

So in a nutshell, how do you re-create or strengthen your MLM blueprint for success?

1) Define and recognize the strengths and challenges of your current blueprint. Do this by completing the questions, writing your historical exposures, and using the ongoing-exposure checklist to analyze your blueprint for strengths and weaknesses.

2) Create an ongoing cleansing process focused on the check-list of ongoing MLM exposures. Accomplish this by doing the following:

   • Be exposed to positive information about our profession. Take ownership of what you allow yourself to be exposed to.

- Be exposed to positive experiences by taking advantage of events and activities provided by your company and your upline leadership.
- Be aware of the three shutdowns and how you can and should respond to them on an ongoing basis.
- Keep the rise-above experiences as your core focus and goal.

CHAPTER 6

Imagination

Up to this point, you have defined and can now recognize the challenges of your current MLM blueprint. You have been exposed to the strengthening process and now understand how it helps you create exposures to support a successful MLM blueprint.

You know the importance of taking control of the thoughts around your MLM experience. You know that what you choose to expose yourself to is what makes the difference. You know where and how to expose yourself to the positivity of this profession. There are a whole lot of feel-good positive facts about this business, and you know how to access them. With the right exposures, you can continually nourish your subconscious, beginning with your imagination, where all thoughts are magnified.

In *Excuse Me, Your Life is Waiting*, Lynn Grabhorn says, "It takes only 16 seconds of focused thought to begin a manifestation. The more intense the emotion behind the thought, the more powerful the whirlwind of energy becomes." This whirlwind of energy is the very thing that creates new imprints. Again, the stronger the emotion behind the thought, the quicker the process happens. The strengthening process creates "do want" positive emotions around the things you desire for your MLM business. It can happen quickly depending on the level of intensity you give it.

The strengthening process is ongoing. It never stops. The challenge lies in taking in new information and experiences about this profession every day. Some information is positive and some is negative, so you need to recognize both as potential exposures on your subconscious. As new experiences come in, use the ones that serve you and correct the ones that don't. And the first place those exposures hit when they enter your subconscious is your imagination.

This book has already exposed you to the vast possibilities of the imagination. We have learned that the imagination magnifies everything we send it, good or bad. Anything you can do to nourish your imagination in a positive way will help you manifest positivity.

When you were a child, your imagination ran wild with possibility. You believed you could do anything. We can learn so much by watching young children—the way they are captivated by colorful books, how they use crayons and coloring books, the way they play with their toys, and how they interact with other children.

They are excited. You can see how their imagination drives them. Children grow and develop at a rapid pace because of the way they utilize their imagination. As we grow older, we are trained to utilize our conscious thought process. We live more in the conscious, logical world, while children live more in the subconscious, imaginative world.

Obviously there is a need for both, but adults tend to forsake their imaginations for a more logical approach. I am amazed as I watch the majority of people coming into my seminars and workshops who want to bypass personal development training and go straight to the logical *how-tos* for doing the business. This is a huge mistake because most people coming in exist in a highly negative world. Their subconscious blueprinting is not ready for or is not aligned for success. They will pay thousands of dollars for training materials bearing titles like:

- Learn how to recruit
- What to do when you exhaust your warm market
- Seven steps to building a massive downline
- The 50 best scripts to closing the sale
- Five daily activities that will guarantee a six-figure income in MLM

I just made up these titles, but there are hundreds of actual titles like these, and new people in this profession flock to them. Some of those trainings are quite good, and I recommend many of them. However, until your subconscious, beginning with your imagination, is in alignment with your desires, you will be blocked from having much success.

My challenge to you is **to get back to the core of where everything happens**. Focus on personal development training that helps you understand how to utilize your subconscious—after all, it's in the subconscious where all things manifest. The stories in your mind truly do become the stories of your life.

So what can you do to positively nourish the imagination? There are three primary nourishments that will create a vibrant and strong imagination for success. Each of them has already been mentioned in this book, but now we'll explore them in more detail. I am astonished at the power these three nourishments provide to the subconscious, and I attribute my success in this profession, and in my life, to mastering these nourishments:

1) Affirmations or "I am" statements
2) Visualization
3) Everyday language

Often, people feel (or say) affirmations do not work for them. The two most common flaws people bring to their affirmation efforts are:

1) They don't visualize or don't fully understand the power and importance of the visualization process.

2) Their everyday language, usually negative, cancels out their desired affirmation with more dominant negative ones.

Fortunately, exercising your imagination can correct this.

AFFIRMATIONS (OR "I AM" STATEMENTS)

Imagination exercises are extremely powerful because they speak directly to the subconscious with highly positive imprinting. The subconscious immediately begins to manifest these things into your life, even though they exist primarily in your imagination now. I cannot begin to tell you how many "ideal days" I have actually lived after thinking of them or writing down the details several months or years before. Putting these dreams into words will put you on the path to realizing your goals.

There is a wealth of information available about the positives of the MLM profession. If you want to be successful in this business, you need to treat it like a business. Study the industry, read books about the industry, and subscribe to magazines that highlight the network marketing profession. Nourish your subconscious with positive and accurate information.

Let's continue with powerful statements of affirmation. Examples:

1) "I am" statements specifically for your MLM business

2) MLM blueprint statements: This is your official declaration where you stake your claim as a network marketing

professional and a crusader for the greatest profession on the planet.

3) Your ideal network marketing day: This is a powerful exposure for your imagination.

Your "I am" statements written specifically for your MLM business tell yourself these things:

- *I am enjoying an income of $100,000 per month in my network marketing business.*
- *I am a top leader and trainer in my company.*
- *I enjoy helping thousands of people around the globe live their dreams.*
- *I am lucky.*
- *I am attracting business leaders into my downline.*
- *I am attracting the right people into my business.*
- *I am consistently recruiting front line, and my teams are duplicating.*

After analyzing your historical exposures, you can use "I am" statements like these to re-create an MLM blueprint for success. You have seen examples of these in this book. You absolutely will manifest your most consistent "I am" statements. The ones you desire need to become more consistent and more dominant than the ones you don't.

With your MLM specific "I am" statements, it's a good idea to summarize them into one dominant "I am" statement about your MLM business. You also want to clearly state the *why* behind that statement.

EXAMPLE DOMINANT MLM "I AM" STATEMENT

I have earned the top rank in my company and enjoy helping thousands of people live their dreams. Why? I was born to inspire people and to build lasting memories with my family. My business allows me to do both.

The most powerful imagination exercise of all is creating the affirmation or "I am" statement. Every success I am experiencing today is a direct result of a list of "I am" statements I wrote down on four index cards about six years before this writing. The power of the "I am" is that you already *are* the statements you write down.

MLM BLUEPRINT STATEMENT

Your official declaration (use mine until you write your own):

KODY'S NETWORK MARKETING (MLM) BLUEPRINT STATEMENT

Network marketing provides me with a unique opportunity to create a business with LOW START-UP COSTS and with VERY LITTLE RISK. I can work it PART-TIME until it takes over the income I receive from a job. I can build a RECESSION-PROOF business with NO EMPLOYEES, NO OVERHEAD, and NO INVENTORIES. I am in business for myself but have MANY OTHERS who have a VESTED INTEREST in my SUCCESS. I can LIVE and work ANYWHERE I WANT, always be around POSITIVE PEOPLE, and have an ongoing PERSONAL DEVELOPMENT PLAN. I can do what I want, when I want, where I want, and enjoy an adventurous LIFESTYLE. I can create FINANCIAL SECURITY and show others how to do the same. I can HELP OTHERS live a better life with a business that is no respecter of persons, meaning they can come from Yale or they can come from jail and still see success. My business plays no favorites. It treats everyone the SAME but rewards those who PERFORM.

I AM NETWORK MARKETING

By writing this distinct statement, you are now armed with powerful information that you can expose to your subconscious continually. It is this type of statement that will get your imagination working in your favor.

YOUR IDEAL NETWORK MARKETING DAY

Another powerful exercise is to write out your "ideal network marketing day." Then claim it and manifest it. This is mine:

> *I get up in the morning when I decide to get up; I threw away the alarm clock a long time ago. However, I naturally get up early because I am excited about my day. I'm excited about every day. I happen to be staying at my beach residence in Ft. Lauderdale, Florida. I wake to the sounds and smells of the ocean. It is very relaxing. I go for a quick jog on the beach and bask in the morning sunlight. I come back and have a light breakfast with my wife on the porch facing the ocean.*
>
> *I take two hours and work on my next writing project prior to checking any emails or taking any calls. I do a couple conference calls, and I am really excited about the subjects we are discussing. I spend some time with my assistants planning the next leadership retreat—we have some amazing personal development exercises in the works. My wife calls the pilot and schedules the private plane for 4 p.m. We fly to Idaho Falls, Idaho, where our daughter and son-in-law pick us up at the airport. They take us to our mountain cabin in Island Park, Idaho, where the rest of the family is gathered. We have a fun weekend planned, riding snowmobiles and chilling at the cabin.*

Now I wrote this ideal day without thinking too much about it. In fact, it took me seven minutes to write it. I simply allowed my imagination to do the writing. I encourage people to keep a journal and do this exercise often. Obviously, you could have numerous ideal days, and they might all look different

Imagination exercises are extremely powerful because they speak directly to the subconscious with highly positive imprinting. The subconscious immediately begins to manifest these things into your life. I cannot begin to tell you how many "ideal days" I have actually lived after thinking of them or writing them down several months or years before.

POWER OF "I AM"

I always like to illustrate the power of "I am" statements with the story of my dog Gus, a beautiful black Lab who loves to play fetch. I love to walk into the back yard bouncing a tennis ball. When Gus sees that ball, he goes crazy. He knows if I am bouncing a tennis ball in front of him, it won't be long before I throw it out in the yard for him to fetch. He will look up with his happy eyes, furiously wave his tail back and forth, and impatiently wait for the fun to begin. I throw that tennis ball out to the far end of the yard, and Gus takes off on a dead run and snatches that ball in his mouth as fast as he can. He always runs right back to me with the prize. When he gets back to me, he does not like to let go of the ball; in fact, I have to pry it out of his mouth. Usually when I do, he has managed to slobber all over the ball. I take that grimy ball and throw it out in the yard again. The slobbery ball lands in dirt, and the dirt sticks on the ball. So now it's grimy, slobbery, and dirty. Gus doesn't care. He snatches up that ball in his mouth and comes running back to me for more.

By this point in the game, I like to bring out a brand new tennis ball. Gus will come back with the old grimy ball in his mouth and see that I have a new one. He is so excited at the possibility of getting his jaws around that new ball. I bounce it in front of him, and he watches with the old grimy ball still in his mouth. I finally throw that ball out in the yard, and he runs to it as fast as he can. When he gets to the ball, he will stop, look down at the new ball, look back at me, look back down at the new ball, and wonder what to do. He refuses to let go of the old tennis ball, so he cannot figure out how to pick up the new one. In his confusion, he will lie down next to the new ball, and the game is over.

Now before you start calling Gus a crazy or dumb dog, I challenge you to consider how you might be doing something very similar in your own life. How often do we see new opportunities come our way and get excited about those opportunities but find ourselves unable to take advantage because we are hanging onto some old tennis ball or old limiting belief? What are some old tennis balls keeping you from living your full potential? The old tennis balls in our life show up as excuses, limiting beliefs, and plain old stinking thinking—phrases like, I*'m too old to start something new, I don't deserve it, I'm not good at new technology, I don't know the right people, I can't get a break because things are too political, I didn't get in on the ground floor, I'm not smart enough, I don't have the time, it takes money to make money, people are out to get me, I can't trust anyone, it wasn't meant to be, or the best one of all,* **I must accept my fate!**

Excuse me, I need to stop writing for a second so I can go take a shower. I feel dirty after writing that last paragraph. That is some of the dirtiest language anyone can think, let alone write. Those things are nothing more than old dirty, grimy, slimy, ugly tennis balls. If we are hanging on to them, we cannot accept, let alone pick up, the new ones when they are thrown for us. It seems silly that we hang on to the old tennis balls, those limiting beliefs that dramatically hold us back. Why do we cling to those grimy tennis balls, and where did they come from?

Somewhere along the line, we started allowing these excuses and limiting beliefs to enter our subconscious. They started showing up in the language we use every day. We started to say we had problems instead of challenges. We started to consistently use words like *can't, try, don't, no, never, realistic*, and any other limiting word that created grimy, ugly tennis balls. The more we used this language, the more we subconsciously suffered. This didn't happen overnight. It took years, and slowly but surely we started heading our mindset in the wrong direction.

So how do we turn this around? How do we change this kind of thinking? I suggest we go back to our dogs, who teach us valuable lessons about life. The only way I can get Gus to let go of the old grimy tennis ball in his mouth is to throw the new one over and over and over again. If I keep doing this, eventually he will drop the old tennis ball and pick up the new one. So how do we throw ourselves the new tennis balls? We do it the same way we created the old ones, but in a faster, more creative, and more productive way. We simply create the statements we desire in present tense and start throwing those messages to ourselves over and over again.

This is where "I am" statements come into play. Remember your subconscious does not know the difference between what is real or imagined, so if you state in present tense the things you desire, your subconscious says, "OK." It accepts whatever you send it as if it already exists.

Now where do you suppose this messaging is being sent? Those statements land directly on the imagination. There they are magnified, and beliefs and habits begin to form to support the message.

If you don't believe this, think of all the negative statements you have been sending to yourself, many times without even knowing it. As an example, if you have been saying, "I can't afford it," guess what? You are right. Your imagination magnifies that statement, your subconscious says, "OK," and it delivers exactly what you have been sending it. You *can't* afford it. Without even knowing it, you have been throwing out an "I am" statement that says, "I can't afford it." The problem is obvious. That negative statement created a negative belief, formed negative habits, and produced a negative result.

In my own life, I replaced this statement with many new ones, such as, "I am attracting wealth in abundance," "I am financially independent and free," and "I am a money magnet." Amazing things have happened in my financial life since I started throwing these new statements to my subconscious over and over and over again. In addition, I make a point to get rid of any negative language in my life. You will never hear me say, "I can't afford it." I will say things like, "I choose not to spend my money on that at this time." See the difference? This keeps a positive message about money flowing to your subconscious. These principles apply to any area in your life.

There is one thing I can absolutely promise you: Your imagination will love chewing on positive "I am" statements you throw to it. Simply write them down and read them out loud, over and over again. Your imagination will magnify them. It's important to remember that your most dominant statements—meaning the ones you use the most—will always win. Most affirmations don't work because people let their daily language overpower the affirmations they wrote down. In other words, they absolutely are manifesting their "I am" statements; it just so happens that the ones they are saying, often without even knowing it, are the negative "I am" statements they don't want.

VISUALIZATION

Go back to the examples of looking at life through the lens of a child. They are masters of visualization. They love to color, draw, and look at pictures. As adults, we too can still visualize our desires in many ways.

I have often said I can tell you what someone will possess in five years based on the magazines they subscribe to. For 20 years, I have subscribed to *Dirt Wheels* Magazine (off-road four-wheelers), *SnoWest* (mountain snowmobiles), *Iron Horse Magazine* (Harley-Davidson motorcycles), and other similar publications. If you walk into my shop, you will see four-wheelers, Harley-Davidson motorcycles, and snowmobiles. Visualization is one of the most powerful things we have to nourish our imaginations. I encourage people to write down an "I am" statement and then visualize and reinforce it with pictures. Again, it also helps to state why it is that you desire what you are visualizing.

For many years, I have been in love with Aston Martin cars. During a financially challenging time of my life, I wrote down an "I am" statement that said, "I am enjoying my new Aston Martin V8 Vantage." I added statements as to why I loved that car, and I took a picture of me next to one on the showroom floor of a dealership. I had that image and statement printed onto a card and carried it around with me for two years. At the end of those two years, I walked into a dealership and purchased a shiny new Aston Martin V8 Vantage. That became a popular story within our company. I owned the car for about two years and then gave it away in a contest sponsored by my company. We had lots of fun with it. (Just a quick side note: These fun contents and giveaways are the sort of thing you see in our profession all the time.)

After giving away the car, I really got into my Harleys, so I didn't really think much about missing the car. However, Aston Martin continued to send me their magazine in the mail every three months. I love looking at this magazine. It has the style of the *Robb Report*, featuring affluent lifestyles. It also highlights Aston Martin cars as part of that lifestyle. In reading this magazine, I was exposed to the new Aston Martin cars, and one of the cars commonly featured was a metallic white V12 Vantage. This is the most beautiful model and color they make. I decided if I were ever to buy another Aston Martin, that would be it.

Shortly after receiving one of these magazines, our family took a weekend trip to Disneyland, where we all ran in the Disney 5K race together. We flew into the John Wayne airport and then had lunch in Newport Beach. On the way from there to Disneyland for the 5K, we passed the Newport Beach Aston Martin dealership. We all wanted to come back and check out the new cars, but we never did make it back that weekend.

But a seed was planted. When we got back to Utah, I looked up Aston Martin Las Vegas, since I was going to Vegas the next day on business. Their website showed that just two days prior, they had received a new metallic white V12 Vantage at their store. I really didn't think much of it, other than that I was going to stop by and check it out. The last thing on my mind was buying a new car. When I got to the dealership the next day, I took one look at that car and knew I was in trouble. I drove the car, and I was in more trouble. But nothing could have prepared me for what happened next.

Most of you who know me know I love rap music, and I write and perform raps with positive messages. I had written and performed, throughout the previous year, a song that had the following lyrics:

> *Cruise the coast into Malibu*
> *Another cool place where the private jet flew*
> *Dining at the Pelican a matter of choice*
> *Parking up the Aston by the Phantom Rolls Royce.*

The next day, I came back to the dealership with my wife Jodi. They had moved the white V12 Aston Martin into the showroom floor. It was parked next to a black Phantom Rolls Royce. *Parking up the Aston by the Phantom Rolls Royce.* They were the only two cars on the showroom floor. How do you have all that happen to you and finish the story without buying the car? Needless to say, I am the proud owner of a new Aston Martin V12 vantage.

This is manifestation at its very best. My imagination was nourished with a rap song (words or statements) and a magazine (images of white Astons and affluent lifestyles). It is this amazing profession that gives me the freedom and resources to experience things like this.

I encourage you to take the whole visualization process seriously. Visualize your goals and dreams with images. If you desire a lifestyle of freedom and affluence from your network marketing business, visualize and reinforce that lifestyle with photos and statements. With today's technology, you can do an Internet search for any image you want and have access to multiple photos in seconds. Use the technology. Print posters with those images, make yourself cards with those images, and create screensavers on your computer. Have fun. Use your imagination. Be a kid again. I triple-dog-dare you.

EVERYDAY LANGUAGE

Take control of your everyday language—it might sound simple, but it is hugely important. Make sure your everyday language is in alignment with these positive statements you are attempting to imprint on your subconscious.

If you are going to write down "I am" statements and visualize them, check your daily language. Make a conscious effort to catch yourself when you use language that cancels out your "I am" statement. If you write down a statement like, "I am financially independent and free," you can never use daily language that says, "I can't afford to buy a new car." If it's not the right time to buy that new car, you would say, "I choose to invest my money on other things at this time."

If you write down a statement like, "I am enjoying an income of $100,000 per month in my network marketing business," you can never use daily language that says, "There are only a lucky few in this business who ever make that kind of money."

If you write down a statement like, "I am a top leader and trainer in my company," you can never use daily language that says, "I wish I could lead and train my people like so-and-so."

If you write down a statement like, "I am attracting business leaders into my downline," you can never use daily language that says, "I can't seem to find people who will duplicate my efforts."

If you write down a statement like, "I am consistently recruiting front-line, and my teams are duplicating," you can never use daily language that says, "Recruiting is a pain, and I wish the people on my team would do what I tell them to do."

I hope you get the point. Your imagination will magnify your most dominant thoughts and images. The beliefs and habits supporting your most dominant thoughts and images will naturally develop. Together, these make up the workings of your subconscious, where all things are manifested.

The language you use is a very important part of this ongoing process. Words represent power. They evoke emotion, good or bad. Words convey your thoughts to the subconscious. They also initiate more thoughts. For your MLM blueprint to serve you successfully, you need to take a close inventory of the words you use to describe your business and the words you use to describe your daily experiences in this profession.

WORDS THAT DESCRIBE YOUR BUSINESS

To this point, we have been referring to the profession predominantly as MLM. The title of this book is *MLM Blueprint*. There is a reason this title was chosen over the alternate title of the profession—network marketing. Remember, the purpose of this book is to recognize negative imprints on the subconscious, replace them with positive imprints, and re-establish a blueprint for success.

MLM is an acronym for multilevel marketing. Studies show that the term *MLM* stirs more emotional negativity than the other title. For this reason, we call the book, the workshop, and the entire study *MLM Blueprint*. We want to invoke your emotions and get to the core of any negative imprinting challenging you.

Now analyze the acronym *MLM*. Are you involved with the MLM profession or the network marketing profession? Read these descriptions and choose which sounds more professional to you: "I am in the MLM business," or "I am in the network marketing business." Which term is most likely to trigger feel-good emotions? Most people give the answer, "I am in the network marketing business." Most people feel this statement is more professional and credible than saying they are "in an MLM." There is no right or wrong answer to this. Use the statement that resonates most with you. The people you approach about getting into your business do not make decisions based on what you say or do; they make decisions based on how you make them feel. When you mention "what you do," referring to MLM or network marketing, always choose the term you can say with the greatest amount of enthusiasm.

The term you choose will be the term you will **always** use when referring to the type of business you are in. With your answer to this simple question, you can quickly change your vibrational energy around your MLM or network marketing business.

Analyze the word *industry*. Are you involved with an industry or a profession? Which word is most likely to trigger feel-good emotions?

Compare these statements:

- I'm involved with the network marketing *industry*.

versus

- I'm in the network marketing *profession*.

I remember the first time I was approached with the difference between these two words. In my speeches and trainings, I was referring to our business with the word *industry*. I was saying things like, "We are in the greatest industry in the world," or "It's time to get excited about this industry."

At one of my events, a member of the audience approached me after my speech and said, "Kody, you need to refer to this business as a *profession*, not an *industry*." At the time, I blew it off. In fact, I walked away from him and thought to myself, "Whatever, dude." I really didn't think there was a difference at all. He must have gotten my attention, however, because I kept thinking about his comment. I decided that for the next week, I would use the word *profession* every time I referred to our business. While doing this, I noticed people in our business who used the word industry, and I noticed people who used the word *profession*.

Within one week, I was astounded at the difference. Using the word *profession* evoked far more powerful emotion for me than the word *industry*. I felt better—more professional. I noticed others feeling the same way. My close friend Eric Worre, owner of Network Marketing Pro, has opted for the word *profession* for years. He has trained hundreds of thousands of people about this profession and has become one of the top crusaders for it in the world. There is an amazing energy around his message. When you finish listening to him, you are convinced that the network marketing profession, though not perfect, is better than any other income-generating opportunity available. The key language he uses is the word *profession*.

WORDS THAT DESCRIBE DAILY EXPERIENCES IN THE BUSINESS

Analyze the word *prospecting*.

Are you *prospecting* with people or *sharing* with people? Which word is most likely to trigger feel-good emotions?

When you say the word *prospect*, you immediately think and feel that you are selling that person something.

When you say the word *share*, you immediately think you have something to offer that will improve someone's quality of life.

Which of these feels better to you? As soon as you hold the belief that your network marketing opportunity provides a better quality of life for others, you will understand that you simply share that opportunity with those who are ready. You implement the law of averages and share with as many people as you can. You detach from the outcome of your sharing efforts, focusing on the activity itself. This takes off all the pressure and helps you maintain the positive energy you need during your daily activities.

One simple word change—from *prospecting* to *sharing*—and you begin sending exposures to the subconscious that serve your business in a positive way.

ANALYZE THE WORDS "CLOSE," "SIGN UP," AND "SPONSOR"

Are you *closing* or *signing up* someone, or are you *sponsoring* them? Which words are most likely to trigger feel-good emotions?

When you use the words *close* or *sign-up*, again you immediately think and feel that you are in sales and under pressure to close the deal.

When you use the word *sponsor*, you are in the mindset of being a coach or a helper to people who want a positive change in their lives.

As soon as you understand the essence of the word *sponsor*, you begin to understand the dynamics that make this profession so amazing. A sponsor is someone who genuinely cares for the person sponsored, who will nurture and coach the new person along until the new distributor learns how to do things on his or her own. Sponsors in this profession wants to see the person sponsored succeed at or beyond the sponsor's own level. This is the only profession I know of that has that kind of motivation built in. Why? Because in this profession, the success of others always elevates your own. When you talk about wanting to "sign someone up" or "close" them, you naturally think in terms of "how much money can this person make me?" When you wish to *sponsor* someone, you naturally think in terms of bringing someone into the profession and helping them reach a new level of prosperity.

Sponsor is one of the key words in the training materials provided by my company. We refer to the daily activities as *list*, *share*, and *sponsor*. We suggest that our distributors make a *list* of contacts and always be adding to that list, *share* the products and opportunity you have to offer, and *sponsor* those who are ready and understand what it means to be a sponsor. Using this type of language, our distributors are able to improve the words they use to describe the daily activities of their network marketing business.

The language you dominantly use in your life and in this business will have a direct effect on what you manifest. Remember your subconscious does not think—it feels. Those feelings, good or bad, come from the language you use. After all, language is the communication tool of the conscious mind. If you look at the blueprint of your mind, you can see how this process works.

Everything begins with an experience from your conscious world. Those experiences are communicated to you with language or words. You process those words with your own thoughts, and you communicate to your subconscious, beginning with your imagination and with your own language. Sometimes the communication is written ("I am" statements), other times it is spoken (daily language), and most often, it is thought. By making a conscious effort to enhance the language you use daily, and by making sure your daily language is in alignment with your "I am" statements, you dramatically improve the exposures that imprint your subconscious.

We have now explored the vast power of the imagination and the daily language we expose to it. Based upon this, your beliefs and habits are layered, and the all-powerful manifestation process takes place.

CONSCIOUS

Things you see

LIFESTYLE

EXPERIENCES

INFORMATION

HABITS

BELIEFS

IMAGINATION

SUBCONSCIOUS

Things you
do not see

CHAPTER 7

Beliefs

We now understand the power of the imagination. We know it magnifies whatever thought or image we send it. We know the imagination is the foundational blueprint upon which our beliefs and habits are built. Beliefs are at the core or center of your subconscious activity. They have power beyond measure. Your beliefs are a natural byproduct of what's happening in your imagination.

It's time to take inventory of your beliefs. A list of your beliefs will help you see what kind of subconscious blueprint you have created over the years. The key is to have more positive beliefs than negative ones. If you don't, you can work on your beliefs until you do.

One of my "I am" statements says, "I am a believer." I have found that it is much better to focus on what you believe in rather than what you *don't* believe in. Belief creates possibility, it renders hope, and it delivers an abundance of energy. Non-belief creates doubt, it renders negativity, and it depletes our energy.

Along with this, it is important to be *pro* something rather than *anti* anything. Being *for* something keeps you in the positive state of belief. Being *against* something keeps you in the negative state of non-belief. The last thing I want to do is get political: I believe we all have a right to believe in and support whatever we want or like as long as it does not cause harm to others.

My suggestion is that we stay on the positive side of what we support rather than on the negative side of what we don't support.

Be a believer and stand strong on the positive side of what you have a passion for. The best way to do this is to keep yourself in the spirit of believing.

I have a list of things I believe in; I encourage you to write your own list. This is one of the most powerful ways to tap into the workings of your subconscious. Your beliefs represent who you are. Here is my list:

I am a believer.

I believe there is a lot more good in the world than bad.

I believe you can do anything you set your mind to.

I believe we are all created equal, yet we are all unique.

I believe everyone has something only they can contribute to the world.

I believe love and gratitude are the two greatest forces in the universe.

I believe you deserve and you will receive exactly what you send out.

I believe written expressions create an energy that makes our world a better place.

I believe a picture is worth a thousand words.

I believe a prompting is a gift that must be acted upon.

I believe life is an adventure and should be lived with passion.

I believe in a person's right to follow his or her heart, and those who do show great courage.

I believe in respecting others' right to believe as they choose.

I believe faith and love will deliver a life of abundance.

I believe in living "happily ever after."

I believe friendship is what life is all about.

I believe my friends are the best people in the world.

I believe crystals in freshly fallen snow are the most beautiful sight in the world.

I believe an ocean beach is a magical place where you can dream and feel at peace.

I believe life is a collection of stories.

I believe wealth is available in abundance.

I believe every year will be a year of wonderful stories and abundant prosperity.

I believe miracles come from the goodness of people's hearts.

I believe in Jesus Christ, and I cherish the annual celebration of his birth.

I believe it is OK to tell you what I believe because I respect you for what you believe.

I believe all mankind has a desire to love and be loved, and that is all we really need to know.

I believe we can all reflect on the power of believing. It's important to believe in good things, to know that our world is filled with hope and that we can make a difference and bring great joy to others. I believe prayers are answered, especially when people choose to be an answer to the prayers of others.

CONCEIVE IT, BELIEVE IT, ACHIEVE IT

Napoleon Hill, in his classic book *Think and Grow Rich*, writes, "What the mind of man can conceive and believe, it can achieve." He also mentions, "Faith is the starting point for all accumulations. Faith is the basis of all miracles and all mysteries, which cannot be analyzed by the rules of science. Faith is the only known antidote for failure." Those are powerful words from one of the greatest personal development instructors in history.

If you believe in greatness, then you will attract greatness. If you believe in abundance, then you will attract abundance. If you believe there is far more good in the world than bad, then you will attract the good into your life.

I challenge you to believe in greatness. Write your list of positive beliefs. Add to that list whenever a new thought comes to you. This will put you in the positive mindset of believing. This is where greatness happens.

In the documentary film *What the Bleep Do We Know?*, there are many concepts shared about belief patterns and how they shape our lives. Here are some of the notes I took while watching this film:

"We only see what we believe is possible. What we believe is possible is based on our conditioning. Our conditioning creates our beliefs about ourselves and others. We do not see others, the world, or ourselves with our eyes. We literally see what we believe we see. We see what we tell ourselves."

The conditioning mentioned in the film has been explained in detail in this book. Our exposures or experiences from our environment generate thoughts. Those thoughts are communicated with our language. Our language evokes emotions that either feel good or bad. Our emotions imprint the exposure on our subconscious, starting with our imagination where those thoughts and emotions are magnified. Thus, our conditioning, or this process, creates our beliefs, and we literally believe what we see in our imagination.

In the same film, Dr. Joseph Dispenza shared the concept that because our beliefs are what we see, we can create any reality we desire. With this knowledge, he wakes up in the morning and consciously creates his day the way he wants it to happen. This is a powerful concept. Many call this segment "intending." This is where you visualize your day or an activity in your day the way you would like to see it happen. You state in present tense the way you see the experience happening.

What you are doing is conditioning your mind to believe that a reality you desire is happening. Most of the time, we allow pre-conditioning to determine a reality that we don't desire. Talk about the power of what we believe in! Remember, the subconscious does not know the difference between what is real or imagined. The stories we see in our mind are the stories we live in our life.

If you focus on your list of positive beliefs, you are in the mindset and vibrational energy to manifest positive things in your life. With this mindset, you can do what Dr. Dispenza describes. You can create your day, your weeks, your months, and your years the way you want them to happen. You can do this in all areas of your life, and you certainly can do it in your network marketing business.

There are three belief activities you can do to strengthen these blueprints. As you complete these activities, you will nourish the imagination and begin the habit of creating beliefs that serve your purpose.

1) Write down a list of your positive beliefs (see page 106 for my examples). This will put you in the positive-belief mindset.

2) Write down a list of positive beliefs specific to your network marketing business. Here are some of mine:

   I believe network marketing is the most efficient way to create residual income.

   I believe network marketing creates financial and time freedom.

   I believe the steps to success in this business to be simple and duplicable.

   I believe I can live the life of my dreams using network marketing as my vehicle.

   I believe that by sharing this profession with others, I am helping them live a better life.

   I believe network marketing provides the best environment for personal development.

   I believe in working the law of averages in this business.

   I believe shutdowns in this business can be prepared for and minimized.

   I believe rise-above experiences change lives for good.

   I believe network marketing recognizes peoples' accomplishments better than any other business environment.

   I believe network marketing is a proven vehicle for massive financial success.

   I believe network marketing instills hope, creates possibility, and delivers a method for success.

   I believe network marketing is the great equalizer.

I believe network marketing is the greatest profession for the masses to realize their dreams.

I believe I am attracting the right people into my business.

I believe that sharing is caring.

I believe I am building wealth with my network marketing business.

I believe people on my contact list will love what I have to offer.

I believe sponsoring new representatives is fun and easy.

3) Use "I am" statements to shift negative beliefs into positive beliefs:

Look at the last three beliefs on the list above. Most people do not believe those three things when they first get into this business, even though they need to believe them if they want to succeed. So how can you shift your beliefs?

Let's say you have about one hour per day, six days a week, that you can commit to building your network marketing business (this is possible for most people). Your upline has taught you a system where you:

1)   Create a list of people
2)   Share your product and opportunity
3)   Sponsor and teach people to do the same

Most people are initially intimidated by this profession and automatically believe the people they put on their list will not be interested. They also believe it will be awkward or difficult to share the products and opportunity. And they believe sponsoring people is hard.

We manifest that which we imagine and believe. If your network marketing list of beliefs includes negatives like the ones in the last paragraph, you will manifest that which you imagine and believe. The good news is, you can use "I am" statements to shift these negative beliefs into positive ones.

I am maintaining a list of people I am excited to talk to.

I love sharing the product and opportunity because they both help people.

Sponsoring new representatives is fun and simple. It is my favorite activity.

You can even break those down into manifesting the ***ideal one-hour-per-day*** experience. Remember, the story in your mind becomes the story of your life.

You manifest the ***ideal one-hour-per-day*** by writing it down, thinking it, and believing it before the day arrives:

Example of my ideal ***ideal one-hour-per-day***:

Because I have created the habit of meeting new people, I am adding several people a day to my list, and they love what I have to offer. I share my product and opportunity at least twice a day, and I sponsor a new rep every week. I am having fun because I truly care about the people I talk to. By example, I teach others how to do what I am doing. My one-hour-per-day consists of adding new people to my list, sharing my product and opportunity twice a day, and either sponsoring a new rep or working closely with a rep I already sponsored.

Your subconscious does not know whether you actually had the above experience or not. You simply say it as if it already exists, and it begins to manifest. The result is that you shifted your negative beliefs into the following:

*I believe people on my **list** will love what I have to offer.*

*I believe **sharing** is caring.*

*I believe **sponsoring** new representatives is fun and easy.*

This process is not difficult, especially if you believe it will work for you. If you don't believe it, take my word for it. Ride on my belief and do the activity until it becomes your belief.

A final thought on beliefs: Those who use prayer and meditation as part of their spiritual and personal development quest are believers. Those beliefs come in all shapes and sizes, but they all believe in a "higher source" of some kind.

Being the believer that I am, I have always used prayer as a way to connect with the higher source I believe in. For many years of my life, my prayers consisted of thanking God for some things, and asking for others. For the past five years, I have simply given prayers thanking God for all my blessings, past, present, and future. I believe in a God that is waiting to shower blessings of abundance upon us. We get in the way with our limiting beliefs. Many people are faithful in praying, but block the blessings with the thoughts and words they use. They may say things like, "It would be nice if," "I really need this," or "I don't have that, so what am I going to do?" kind of language in their prayers.

Instead of getting in our own way—or even in God's way—I'd suggest that we simplify the process. Simply pray using words of thanks. I believe in a loving God as my source, and I use prayer to communicate with that source. Whomever or whatever your source is, communicate in the spirit of giving thanks and watch what happens.

Speaking of beliefs:

I believe I am in control of my destiny.

I believe I can do all things through Christ who strengthens me.

I believe it's OK to tell you that because I also respect your positive source.

I believe we are all destined for greatness.

I believe we will be challenged, we will be tested, and we will prevail triumphant.

I believe in a life of abundance and that all things are meant to come together for our good.

I believe in people.

I believe in me.

I believe our purpose is to love and be loved and that our biggest test is in how we break down our differences with others.

I believe we are our greatest asset or our biggest liability. I choose to be an asset in my own life and in the lives of others.

I believe it is time for people to take charge of their lives.

I believe it is time to dust off the dreams you have and make them happen.

I believe every day is an amazing day.

I believe the sun is always shining, even when storms have set in.

I believe that in the darkest moments, the stars appear.

It's time to believe in your purpose and know that you are the best "you" in the history of the world. Conceive it, believe it, and make it happen in your life.

CHAPTER 8

Habits

With the "mind-blueprint" illustration, we can clearly see how everything starts with an experience that comes from our environment. Our thoughts around that experience are elevated or diminished by the language we use. That language either makes us feel good or bad, and it's those emotions that serve like an intensely bright light, placing the exposure on our imagination.

In creating the ideal blueprint for MLM success, we have explored numerous ways to nourish our emotions into a feel-good state around our MLM experience. We have seen how our imagination magnifies our thoughts and emotions, creating beliefs and habits around them. This represents the workings of our subconscious, where all things are manifested.

HABITS

BELIEFS

IMAGINATION

SUBCONSCIOUS

Things you
do not see

After reading this book and understanding the process, hopefully you are becoming trained on how to take control of the exposures creating your subconscious blueprints. You have learned how to create a positive imagination through your "I am" statements" and visualization. You can see how your imagination magnifies that positivity and forms beliefs and habits that support it.

You have learned how to explore your current beliefs, write a list of your positive beliefs—whether real or imagined—and shift negative beliefs to positive ones with "I am" statements and intention. You have seen that by consciously directing your beliefs, you can alter them, which has a positive effect on your imagination and your habits. The fascinating thing about the subconscious is that you can work on any of the three main blueprints (imagination, beliefs, or habits), and they will help the others. They are intertwined—three separate functions but one in purpose.

The habits we form become the bridge between our subconscious and conscious worlds. Habits represent action. These are the things we do consistently, usually without even knowing it. The autopilot aspect of our habits is run by the subconscious; the action itself is run by our conscious mind.

For example, when you get up in the morning, I'll bet the toothpaste is on the toothbrush and in your mouth before you even realize it. You begin brushing your teeth, and your conscious mind kicks in. Habits are created by consistent activity done over time. Some studies have shown it takes a minimum of 28 days of consistent activity for an individual to form a habit, good or bad.

There are four levels to creating a habit:
- Level 1—unconscious incompetence: This is where you don't think about what you don't do.

- Level 2—conscious incompetence: This where you think about what you don't do.
- Level 3—conscious competence: This is where you think about what you do.
- Level 4—unconscious competence: This is where you no longer think about what you do.

It is at Level 4 that your actions become habit. Notice the language. It says that you are acting from a subconscious level. You no longer think about how to tie your shoes; you just tie them. You no longer think about brushing your teeth; you just brush them. You are on autopilot.

Here is a list of Level 4 activities or habits that people should be acquiring in their MLM careers—these are the fundamentals:

1) You no longer think about using the products; you just use them.

2) You no longer think about presenting your opportunity; you just present it.

3) You no longer think about getting on the weekly conference call; you just get on it.

4) You no longer think about listening to a positive CD every morning; you just keep one in your car and listen to it.

5) You no longer think about adding people to your warm-market list; you just meet and add new people to your list.

These are all Level 4 positive habits to building a thriving MLM business. If you are at Level 4 with these five activities, you are in great shape. In fact, the more MLM activities that reach Level 4, the more likely you will maintain a consistent MLM blueprint for success. The glue holding that blueprint together is the habits of the subconscious.

Now, here is the challenge. Most people only get to Level 2 or 3 with their MLM habit formation. This is a fragile place. It's usually here where negativity from others or shutdown experiences prevent people from continuing. Because of this, few people who only dabble in this profession ever get to Level 4 with their MLM activities.

Let's take the five fundamental MLM activities listed above and assume an individual got to Level 3 with each of them:

1) You think about using the products and then use them. While thinking about it, your spouse gives you a hard time about how much the products cost and recommends that you cancel your autoship.

2) You think about the details of presenting your opportunity, but you also think about the rejection you got last week from your best friend and focus instead on the doubt you now feel. You reluctantly present the opportunity, and your prospect feels your reluctance.

3) You think about getting on the weekly conference call, but you think about the sitcom your whole family is sitting down to watch at the same time. You dwell about sacrificing time away from TV instead of taking an opportunity to stay focused on your desired future.

4) You think about getting into the trunk of your car to grab the latest CD you are supposed to listen to. It's too big of a pain, you are in a hurry, and besides, you are in the mood for Howard Stern this morning.

5) You think about adding people to your warm-market list. You are not in the mood to meet anyone new today, and you need to call your downline to make sure they are doing their share anyway.

Getting to Level 4 with these activities is crucial to maintaining a healthy MLM blueprint for success. I would go so far as to say if you learn nothing else from this study, please learn that *positive habit formation is the single most important step to succeeding in this business*. Memorize that last sentence and make it part of your personal development plan. If you did nothing else but that, this book and the *MLM Blueprint Workshop* will be worth every dollar and minute of time you invested in it.

How do you create positive habits? As mentioned earlier, consistent daily effort over time—for at least 28 days—is the key to creating a habit. You must be consistent with a few basic things to create the habits you need. Remember habits are the framing of your mind. If you take the MLM fundamentals proven to work over time and get to Level 4—a habit—with those fundamentals, you will have the framing in place. Your positive blueprint will then stand for generations and can help make you a wealthy person.

What are the MLM fundamentals that should become habits? You will want to get with your company or your upline support team and plug into the system of duplication they have created for you. If that system exists, you want to be very careful to avoid the temptation of reinventing the wheel. One of the biggest mistakes I see in this profession is when an aspiring leader insists he or she can create a better, faster, stronger, and more duplicable system than the one that got them to where they are. There are situations where this may be necessary, but they are the exception, not the rule. If I had to choose between a team of people that consistently plugs into a mediocre system or a team that's on a constant quest for a better system, I'd take the first group any day.

Why? Because that is how important habit formation is. Think about it. If you have several workable MLM fundamentals that have been committed to habit, it becomes very difficult for negative exposures or shutdowns to cause any damage—in fact, it's next to impossible.

I like to use the top income-earner in our company as an example. He focuses on primary fundamentals, he has committed those fundamentals to habit, and he teaches others to do the same. He has created "rock-star income" along with "network marketing freedom" because his habits are solid and he refuses to vary from them.

Consistency of a proven system is better than inconsistent use of a perceived better system. Plug into the system provided by your upline support. I am going to share with you some basic fundamentals that should be committed to Level 4 in any plan. Your company or upline plan may present these in a different order or format. They may even call the activity something slightly different. Just remember to look for the fundamentals and the action steps. After our company created its own system and analyzed hundreds of others proven to work throughout the industry, we have found the following items to be most essential. These three principles and five steps should be committed to Level 4.

THE THREE-PRINCIPLE, FIVE-STEP APPROACH

Three principles:

1) Duplication: Everything you do needs to be something your downline thinks they can do.

2) Consistency: You must be consistent and teach your team by example.

3) Play the law of averages, understand them, and be committed to play them for a minimum of two years.

Five steps:

1) Become a product or your company's product.

2) Invite people to look at the product and opportunity.

Whom to invite: Your warm-market list and anyone you meet that you can add to your warm-market list. *(Note: I'm not going to go into detail about cold-market activities like advertising, list buying, cold calling, social media, and other activities people try to sell you on. The bottom line is that any activity you do to meet people is a way to add someone to your warm-market list. This business is about relationships. There comes a point when someone who is cold needs to become warm, and it takes a relationship to do that.)*

How to invite: This includes the use of tools or a rapport-building and filtering process outlined by your upline mentors.

3) Present: Use tools, meetings, and other duplicable ways to present your company's products and opportunity.

4) Follow-up: The fortune is in the follow-up. Be punctual and professional with your follow-up.

5) Train: Teach your new distributors how to do all of the above.

This is what I love about the three principle, five-step approach:

1) It includes proven MLM fundamentals that have worked over time.

2) It allows for flexibility that leaders can work into the system without jeopardizing the formation of habits.

The top income-earner in our company uses these principles and steps to build his business. He has several leaders on his team who have utilized the flexibility in this system without discrediting what he does and teaches. He *invites* and *presents* in a slightly different manner than some of the other top leaders. They simply choose to use different approaches and tools within the system. But they all *invite*, and they all *present*. The critical thing is to never discredit what another leader is doing; this causes confusion within the team. Confusion is the number-one enemy to consistency and habit formation.

The three-principle, five-step approach allows for flexibility while providing a solid program that is duplicable and habit forming. If you create positive habits, your positive-belief system will stay in place, and you will create exposures that will continually nourish a positive blueprint.

It's interesting to compare a building blueprint to a subconscious blueprint:

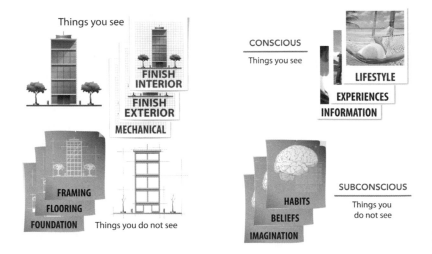

Notice that the *framing* layer is in the same position as the *habit* layer. This further strengthens the analogy, because our habits work just like framing does. Everything we do see in our life is built upon the habits we have formed.

I challenge you to use the building blueprint and subconscious blueprint illustrations as a way to visualize the importance of protecting and developing positive habits. Every time you look at a building structure, visualize the framing behind the structure. Use your imagination to "see" that structure's existence because of the framing under it; transfer that thought to what is going on in your subconscious.

Protect your positive habit formation with all your might. Visualize it as your framing because it is. It will truly make all the difference in the world.

CHAPTER 9

Esteem

Most of us have heard the term *self-esteem*. Most of us immediately think we know its meaning. The dictionary defines *esteem* as, "To value somebody or something highly or to regard something in a particular way." Synonyms for *esteem* are *regard, respect, admiration*, and *good opinion*.

The history of the word gives us insight as to its value. The words *esteem, estimate*, and *aim* all come ultimately from Latin *aestimare*. *Estimate* was a straightforward borrowing from the Latin past participle *aestimatus*, but *esteem* came via Old French *estimer*. Originally, *esteem* meant much the same as the words *estimate, evaluate*, and *assess*. But as early as the 16th century, it had passed into "think highly of."

With that in mind, today's definition would say there is really no such thing as high or low esteem. You either have esteem or you don't. You may have different levels of esteem, but make no mistake, esteem refers only to the positive side of the spectrum. What some would call "low self-esteem" is, in reality, no self-esteem.

Today's definition also implies that you could attach the word *esteem* to anything you desire to "think highly of." We usually see *esteem* attached to the word *self* as in *self-esteem*. Its literal meaning is to "think highly of self." Here is a list of words I see as beautiful companions to the word *esteem*.

Self-esteem	MLM-esteem
Educational-esteem	Money-esteem
Relationship-esteem	Spiritual-esteem
Charitable-esteem	Company-esteem
Organizational-esteem	

The list could go on and on. As esteem pertains to the topic of this book, the two words we need to attach to it are the words *self* and *MLM*. *Self-esteem* and *MLM-esteem* literally mean we think highly of self and we think highly of MLM. You must have both kinds of esteem to thrive in this business.

SELF-ESTEEM

Elevation of self-esteem is essential to creating success in this business. In fact, it may be more essential to success in network marketing than in any other line of work.

Think about it. Network marketing is a business model that requires personal discipline. It is true that you are in business for yourself but not by yourself, but you need to be prepared for the "for yourself" part of this. Most people are highly inexperienced when they start their network marketing careers, and they do it part-time. It starts as *hope* for a better life, then moves to a *possibility* of a plan for that life, and finally graduates to *daily activities* that need to happen. And all of this takes place in one to two hours a day, with a multitude of people telling you what can't be done. In those daily activities, you are faced with rejection and disappointment. Those experiences can be damaging to self-esteem that might be fragile to begin with.

It's great to go to the meetings, be recognized by your company and your peers, listen to motivational messages, and hear the success stories from others who are doing what you are doing. However, there inevitably come days when you are home alone, faced with those daily activities. Your upline does not pick up the phone and make that prospecting call for you. That part is up to you. Your company is not there on the morning when a spouse or family member painfully discourages you. At that moment, you are on your own, and this is where the personal discipline comes in. The top income-earner in your company is not there on the day you realize your promising new front-line recruit quits returning your calls. These are private and very personal moments where you deal with the "for yourself" part of your business.

To handle this, you need to be armed with a healthy and growing self-esteem. This is one of the reasons personal development is so fundamental to our business: It is essential to your success. To establish and nourish a healthy self-esteem, you need a proper plan. With that in mind, I'm going to explain to you why network marketing is the best environment for obtaining that plan. Network marketing is one of the few places where self-esteem nourishment and exercise plans co-exist, and stare you in the face every day.

Self-esteem nourishment comes from an ongoing personal-development plan where positivity is the energy source. Network marketing is a profession where personal development teachers thrive. There are more self-help/motivational books, CDs, seminars, and workshops distributed through the network marketing profession than to any other group or audience. What this means is when you are exposed to network marketing, you will be exposed to a world of positive information most people don't even know exists. You will be encouraged to read a list of positive books, listen to empowering CDs, watch inspiring DVDs, and attend life-changing events, and you will even have opportunities to turn around and teach others the principles you have learned.

Self-esteem exercise comes from daily activity. Those who have something they are building or working toward have a better chance of increasing self-esteem. It's a great thing to be exposed to positivity. It's enhanced tenfold when you can take that positivity every day and apply it to something you are working on.

Network marketing gives you the opportunity to work on something very special for you and your family. The ultimate result is financial and time freedom coupled with adventure, excitement, and fun. Companies and distributors typically have a duplicable system for you to follow that will help you build the lifestyle of your dreams.

Self-esteem nourishment coupled with self-esteem exercises create a strong and vibrant plan for personal development. It's simply not enough to read self-help books or listen to inspirational CDs; you need to attach that positivity to action. Network marketing gives you that action plan along with upline support that coaches you and cheers you on as you advance. As a result, the greatest side benefit to building a network marketing business is that you can get plugged into a highly effective plan that enhances self-esteem.

A strong self-esteem has more control over what it allows to penetrate the subconscious. A strong self-esteem immediately recognizes information and experiences that are not aligned with a strong MLM blueprint. A strong self-esteem takes control and refuses defeat. A strong self-esteem resolves to do more, be better, rise above, and claim victory as a way of life.

There is a scene in the movie *Secretariat* that shows this kind of resolve in action. This movie tells the true story about Secretariat, the horse who did the unthinkable by winning all three Triple Crown events in 1973. As with every great success story, there were days of intense challenge and sacrifice. The owner of the horse was a woman who took over her father's horse ranch after he passed away. Through the turn of some remarkable events, she ended up with a promising new colt she believed would be a champion.

She overcame enormous odds as she held on to the belief that Secretariat had the ability to make history. In trying to raise money to save their ranch, she decided to sell partial breeding rights to the promising race horse, asking a far higher fee than the going rate. Prospective investors said she was acting as if her horse had already won the Triple Crown, and all 42 prospects turned her down. She didn't give up, eventually got funding, and the horse went on to be one of the greatest race horses in history.

If you are in network marketing, you also have something very important to do. Just like the woman who owned Secretariat, you have the opportunity to prove who you really are. You too can take control, refuse defeat, and have the resolve to do more, be better, rise above, and accept victory. You have nothing to prove to anyone except yourself. When you take on this challenge and win, you will come out of the experience with a strengthened self-esteem. You will be able to use that to pursue the next lofty goal on your list.

THE GREATEST MIRACLE

One of my favorite self-help authors is Og Mandino. I recommend you read everything he ever wrote. One of his books is titled *The Greatest Miracle in the World*. Like all of his books, this one is written as entertaining fiction, with time-tested personal development principles taught throughout the story. As you read this book, you soon learn that the greatest miracle in the world is *you*.

If you want to strengthen self-esteem and have the resolve to do something significant, you need to accept the fact that you are, indeed, the greatest miracle in the world. As my nephew Jerame says jokingly, "I am a pretty big deal." I have had the opportunity to coach Jerame and his wife with the principles in this book, and one of the things I asked him to do was to turn that saying from a joke into an actual statement. The statement is "I am a big deal." This is now a message Jerame sends to his subconscious daily to create imprinting for a healthy self-esteem.

Some of you may be reading this and saying, *that is one arrogant or conceited statement*. So it is important that we define what arrogance is. Arrogance is when you put yourself above someone else; it has nothing to do with claiming your greatness. If Jerame were saying, "I am a bigger deal than you," it would be arrogance. He is not saying that. He believes he is a big deal, and he believes you are too, if you claim it.

I remember visiting one of our top distributors in his hometown a few years ago. He picked me up in his car. I got in the passenger side and immediately noticed he had a little sign on his dashboard. It said, "Tommy always wins." If any of you know Tommy, you know he is living that statement. Tommy is a winner, and he is mentoring thousands of others to adopt his creed as their own. He believes everyone can be a winner if he or she claims it.

The top rank in our company is titled "Eagle." There is a story behind that, which has huge sentimental value to myself, my family, and all the distributors in our business. In the early days of our operation before any of our distributors had reached the Eagle rank, our top leaders, along with my wife and family, presented me with the Eagle award. This was a big surprise, since I am the owner; I considered the rank of Eagle to be a sacred honor for distributors who would someday work their way through the ranks. The year before, we had bestowed an honorary Eagle award upon my deceased brother. It is he whom we commemorate by making our top rank Eagle. To have them bestow this honor on me was, indeed, one of the greatest honors I have ever received.

I immediately adopted the title of "Eagle One" as my self-esteem builder. "I am Eagle One." I started sending text messages to my wife every time I landed on an airplane, simply saying, "Eagle One has landed." It seems like a small thing, but those little subtleties send messages to the subconscious and imprint them with the feeling of greatness.

The idea of "Eagle One" has taken on a life of its own for me. Because it's a statement, it manifests itself everywhere I go. My assistant Leann took it upon herself to make sure that when I fly, I always have A1 seating. Why? Because I am Eagle One. I didn't put her up to that; she just did it. Every time I walk on the plane, I smile at the flight attendant and say, "Eagle One is on the plane." She usually gives me a funny look because she has no idea what that means. I know what it means, and that is what matters.

I frequently feel I attract top-class treatment, as if there is a vibrational energy around me. Now before you go off with the arrogance thought, again let me remind you, "I am the greatest miracle in the world." And so are you. "I am an Eagle," and so are you. "I am a big deal," and so are you. "I always win," and so do you. The only thing you have to do is believe it, and you can live it too.

Like my friend Tommy, I am mentoring thousands to take on my aim to become like Eagles in the way they live their daily lives, and there are a number of reasons why I feel people should aspire to this. Eagles are majestic. They provide beauty and direction for all to follow; they inspire with their grace and elegance. Eagles take control, refuse defeat, and have the resolve to do more, be better, rise above, and claim victory. Eagles get what they desire; I believe everyone can live their life like an eagle if they claim it.

When you stake this claim and live this way, you always have not-so-coincidental situations popping up. I have these experiences because I have a self-esteem statement: "I am Eagle One." Tommy has a self-esteem statement: "Tommy always wins." Jerame has a self-esteem statement: "I am a big deal." I encourage you to get yourself a self-esteem statement, one that resonates with you. Claim it, be it, and you will live it.

This simple task will dramatically enhance your self-esteem. You need it, you deserve it, and you must claim it to be successful in this business and in your life. You are the greatest miracle in the world. Every prophetic leader has said this; I think it's time you say it too.

MLM-ESTEEM

Elevation of MLM-esteem is essential to creating success in this business. You've probably already discovered that people love giving you their opinion of MLM, and it is usually negative. As a result, most people walk around with very low MLM-esteem or with no MLM-esteem at all.

Perhaps more than any other industry, MLM is under constant scrutiny and attack by people who know little or nothing about it. Most often, those with uneducated opinions have had an emotionally negative experience or have heard of one from someone close to them. Because of this, their opinions can be very dramatic, loaded with negative energy. As a society, we tend to flock to negativity as a source of entertainment. That is why the verbal and sometimes physically violent talk shows and reality television shows do so well.

As MLM is a word-of-mouth business, its primary source for negative press is also through word of mouth. So its greatest asset can also be its biggest liability. In today's marketplace, people trust word of mouth from those they know and respect far more than they trust any other form of communication, especially about products, services, or opportunities. This is the reason the MLM industry does so well. It's also the reason so many bad opinions are formed. Think about it. People trust word of mouth. As a result, people often take at face value the things they hear about MLM even if its source knows little, if anything, about it. So the state of MLM-esteem in our marketplace is usually low at best and most times nonexistent. The mistake most people make is buying into that negativity. Even those who have positive exposures may allow this kind of talk to rob them of the MLM-esteem they have been able to create.

So how is MLM-esteem elevated? The first few chapters of this book provide an excellent process for creating MLM-esteem. It's important to be educated on MLM blueprints and to discover what your current MLM blueprint looks like. The cleansing process is a necessary step towards creating an MLM-esteem, but it's time for the next level—strengthening that esteem and turning yourself from ordinary to extraordinary.

Again, 90 percent of the equation is about awareness. If we recognize we have an MLM blueprint, know that we must cleanse it, believe that we must strengthen it, pay attention when negative imprints enter, and realize how those imprints attack our MLM-esteem, then we can implement a daily proactive, offensive plan.

As when you're focusing on self-esteem, you will need to be continually armed with facts about the power of MLM-esteem and have ways to stay focused on the power of MLM. Remember *esteem* is "*to think highly of.*" Under all situations, you want to *think highly of* MLM. When you get negative pushback from a prospect, you want to *think highly of* MLM, when you unexpectedly find yourself in a negative conversation about MLM, you want to *think highly* and *speak highly of* MLM. When you are discouraged because your business is not growing the way you want it to, you want to *think highly of* MLM. To do this, you continually go through the same process you do when strengthening your self-esteem. Like your subconscious, your MLM-esteem needs constant nourishment and exercise.

Nourishment comes from an ongoing focus on the positive facts about this business. In Chapter 5, you were given facts about network marketing. Chapter 6 included a powerful MLM statement summarizing the power of this business. The MLM statement is short, precise, and to the point. You can use this statement, or you can write your own. Commit it to memory so you are armed and prepared to share it. There are many times you will want to simply share it with yourself. Other times it will serve as a great speech to others.

There is one very powerful fact about this profession of network marketing that separates it from any other business in the world today. It is this fact that puts the feel-good into our business, which will quiet your internal and external critics faster than anything else. This fact will also silence the criticism behind all the negativity the world throws at the network marketing profession. It is this fact that will strengthen your MLM-esteem if you stay focused on it and use it as your offensive weapon. The fact is this:

MLM is the only profession that exists today that directly and immensely rewards you when you elevate others to a better position in life. Anyone can hold onto any criticism they want about this profession, but they can never argue with this undisputable fact.

I learned about elevating others on a youth group trip my father and I took several years ago. We took several youth from our community for a typical youth outing at Lake Powell in southern Utah. We were there for three days, and we all had lots of fun together, with activities such as waterskiing, tubing, cliff diving, and fireside talks at night. The favorite activity was waterskiing, and all the boys participated. One of the boys was the superstar of the group. He was very athletic and the most popular. Another one of the boys was at the opposite end of the spectrum. He was a little slow, physically challenged, and struggled to connect with the other boys.

When the superstar kid skied, everyone paid attention. He would fly across the wake and shoot huge rooster tails of water as he cut back and forth. Everyone made a big deal over how great this kid skied. When the other boy tried to ski, it was a totally different story. He would get in the water, put two skis on, and proceed to attempt getting up. Time after time, he would try to get up on those skis. Time after time, he failed. This went on for three days. It finally got to the point where the others in the group started to make fun of him.

On the final day, I saw a miracle take place. The other boy, once again, was trying to get up on the skis. After several attempts, the superstar boy stood up in the boat and said he had seen enough of this. He put on his life jacket, jumped into the lake, swam back to the boy, put on the skis, and placed the boy in front of him on the same skis. He told my dad to hit it.

As the boat pulled them forward, the two boys stood up on the skis and proceeded to ski all the way around the cove of that lake. You should have seen the smile on the face of that young man. This was one of those perfect moments, a memory etched into my mind that defined what I aspire to be: Someone who will jump in the lake, swim out to another person in need, put on the skis, and help him get up.

Here is the interesting part of this story: After the two boys finished skiing together, the other boy wanted to attempt getting up one more time on his own. What do you suppose happened? You guessed it. After being shown *how* by another person who cared, he got up on his own on his first attempt. Often, a simple act of caring is all someone needs to get up on their own.

MLM gives us this opportunity like no other profession. We can help people up every day. The challenged boy in this story had physical and mental limitations blocking him from getting up on the skis. There are millions of people around us who are blocked with negative thinking, lack of hope, unseen purpose, feelings of defeat, and feelings of being under-appreciated and even unloved. These same people live in despair, thinking there is no way for them to have a life of prosperity. You might be one of them. There are times in our lives when we are the ones who cannot get up on the skis, and we need help. There are other times when we have the opportunity to jump in the lake and do the helping. Unlike any other business in existence, MLM gives us the mechanism to help and receive help.

CHAPTER 10

Conclusion

Developing the *MLM Blueprint* book and workshop has been an exciting journey. The thoughts, procedures, philosophies, and stories compiled in this book and the *MLM Blueprint Workshop* have taken several years, numerous seminars, and hundreds of coaching sessions to formulate. This is not a simple subject. We have covered the workings of the subconscious, discussed how those workings affect your ability to do this business, and given you proven methods to create a blueprint for massive success.

As a network marketing professional, I challenge you to take full advantage of what this book can do for you. This is not a read-once-and-put-it-on-the-shelf kind of book. This is a book you will want to reference often. The strengthening activities alone will help you clear your mind of all the negativity surrounding this profession. They will help you release the mental blocks that might be holding you back from the success you deserve.

Our ultimate goals are to help individuals in the profession succeed and to elevate the profession as a whole. As you strength en your MLM blueprint, I'd like to encourage you to become crusaders for this profession. Together we can bring a higher level of professionalism to what we do and bring more people into this exciting business.

The philosophy of the MLM blueprint may seem complex, but its process is very simple:

- Use the blueprint illustrations to visualize what is going on in your subconscious mind and understand how that activity manifests in your conscious world.

- Discover your historical exposures to MLM by first answering the questions beginning on page 58. Take your answers and use them to help you discover and write out the *six primary historical exposures* that have had the most impact on your MLM blueprint.

- Use the *ongoing-exposure checklist* as a way to analyze your historical exposures so you can identify your blueprint's strengths and weaknesses (see chapter 3).

- Use the *strengthening activities* (see chapter 5) to create a blueprint that will manifest massive success in this profession.

- Gain a deeper understanding of the workings of your subconscious where all things are manifested (Chapters 6, 7 and 8). In these chapters, you learn amazing facts and simple techniques to help you take control of your imagination, beliefs, and habits.

- Read and re-read the *network marketing (MLM) blueprint statement* provided on page 88.

- Write your own positive *network marketing (MLM) blueprint statement*.

- Write your *ideal network marketing day* (several times in journal entries). See page 89 for an example.

- Write down clear and powerful "I am" statements about your network marketing success. See page 87 for examples.

- Write a dominant "I am" statement about your network marketing business and state your "why" behind that statement. You want to get to the "why" that makes you cry. See page 88 for an example.
- Watch your daily language and recognize when negative statements may be overriding the "I am" statements you've worked so hard to create. This is your daily check to make sure your desired statement is the one that is most used.
- Visualization exercises are always a powerful imprinting process. Take pictures and create dream boards or photo albums. Bring your ideal network marketing dreams alive with visualization.
- Gain an understanding of the word *esteem* and how it can help you become a superstar in your life and in your network marketing career.

I'd like to leave you with a critical message: Take control of your mind. It will help you take control of your network marketing career. Understand that you are in the greatest profession there is for providing residual income. Become engaged in the business-building steps as outlined by your company, your upline, and generic network marketing trainers.

Whether you have an hour a day or you work this business full-time, have a daily plan and understand the importance of consistent action over time. Learn techniques and business-building tips that will keep you from destroying your warm market. By using time-tested methods, you will avoid shutdowns and have people join you and duplicate your efforts at a faster rate.

Learn your company's or upline's systems first and then refer to generic training programs to help you with the proven how-to approaches. Ask your upline to refer you to generic training he or she feels is most conducive to your company approach.

If you and your upline are looking for generic "how-to" training, I recommend Network Marketing Pro. This is a comprehensive website training site established by Eric Worre, who is a seasoned network marketing professional. His generic training products and workshops stick to basic fundamentals that are highly effective. His Recruiting Mastery courses are among the best trainings I have ever seen in this profession. I've had the opportunity to conduct the *MLM Blueprint Workshop* in tandem with his Recruiting Mastery workshop. They work hand in hand, as the blueprint prepares your mindset and the mastery gives you the tools. With the proper tools and techniques for building, you will dramatically enhance your MLM blueprint over time.

The stories you put in your mind are the stories you live in your life. Surround yourself with positive people who have inspirational stories that were created by their network marketing careers. You can find those stories within your own company. Celebrate your top leaders' successes, and soon those successes will become your own.

As you close this book, I'll leave you with my personal development creed, a statement of commitment and a claim on the success that is waiting for you.

MY PERSONAL DEVELOPMENT CREED

Today is the day I will rise to the greatness in me.

Today I choose to:

Accept possibility

Embrace challenges

Respect change

Be consistent

Stay humble

Take responsibility

Choose happiness

Have confidence and

Claim victory.

Today I choose to take control, refuse defeat, and have the resolve to do more, be better, rise above, and accept winning as a way of life.

I am a winner.

I am a voice of difference.

I am a messenger of hope.

I am a leader of possibility.

I am a solution to *freedom*.

I am a crusader for that which is good in the world.

About the Author

Author Kody Bateman is the founder and CEO of a global network marketing company, which was recently featured in the Inc. 500 list as one of the fastest-growing companies in the U.S. Kody is a best-selling author and visionary leader who is living his dream and travels the world teaching others to do the same. Kody has anchored his network marketing company with an ongoing personal development event. Over the past eight years he has personally conducted that event for sold-out audiences throughout the United States, Canada, and Australia. He teaches that the activities of your subconscious must be in alignment with your conscious desires in order to succeed. Kody believes everyone has an MLM blueprint in their subconscious, which either propels them to success or holds them in failure. This book is poised to help millions of people discover their own MLM blueprints, and help them learn how to massively strengthen them to live the life of their dreams.

For more information and updates visit www.mlmblueprint.com.